Cambridge Practice Tests for First Certificate 1 & 2

TEACHER'S BOOK

Paul Carne
Louise Hashemi and
Barbara Thomas

CAMBRIDGE
UNIVERSITY PRESS

PUBLISHED BY THE PRESS SYNDICATE OF THE UNIVERSITY OF CAMBRIDGE
The Pitt Building, Trumpington Street, Cambridge, United Kingdom

CAMBRIDGE UNIVERSITY PRESS
The Edinburgh Building, Cambridge CB2 2RU, UK
40 West 20th Street, New York, NY 10011–4211, USA
10 Stamford Road, Oakleigh, VIC 3166, Australia
Ruiz de Alarcón 13, 28014 Madrid, Spain
Dock House, The Waterfront, Cape Town 8001, South Africa

http://www.cambridge.org

First published 2000
Reprinted 2000

Printed in the United Kingdom at the University Press, Cambridge

Typeface 10.5/12pt Sabon   *System* QuarkXPress® SE

ISBN 0 521 77422 5 Student's Book 1 & 2
ISBN 0 521 77423 3 Teacher's Book 1 & 2
ISBN 0 521 49898 8 Cassette Set (Book 1)
ISBN 0 521 49902 X Casette Set (Book 2)

Contents

Introduction

The First Certificate in English

The First Certificate in English (FCE) is an examination offered by the University of Cambridge Local Examinations Syndicate. It is the most widely taken of their exams. Since it was first offered in 1939 as the Lower Certificate of Proficiency, it has been revised three times – in 1974, in 1984 and, most recently, in 1996. Significant changes were made in 1996. They involved the introduction of new question types and procedures while keeping the level and overall rationale the same. This set of Practice Tests contains material which mirrors the actual exams offered from 1996 and provides valuable information and practice for the five papers of the FCE.

For further information about UCLES exams, write to UCLES, 1 Hills Road, Cambridge, CB1 2EU, England.

Level

Students who pass FCE are expected to be able to function independently in the language in a range of situations. They are able to use and understand the main structures of English and a wide range of vocabulary, and are able to communicate in a range of social situations. A student who passes FCE should be ready to begin using English in a work environment or as a means of study.

On average, a student will be ready to take FCE after approximately 550 hours of active study of English. This obviously varies from person to person depending on their circumstances, ability, motivation, etc., but it is a rough guide.

FCE fits between the Preliminary English Test (PET) and the Certificate in Advanced English (CAE) in the suite of exams which are offered by the University of Cambridge Local Examinations Syndicate. Students who have passed PET could expect to need approximately another 200 hours of active study before they might pass FCE. (In level, PET is about two-thirds of the way to FCE.)

In addition to the required level in English, a student taking FCE needs to have the capacity to survive in the exam room as there are five papers, at least three of which are taken in one day. This requires concentration and staying power.

Structure of the examination

Paper 1	Reading	1 hour 15 mins	four texts – 35 questions
Paper 2	Writing	1 hour 30 mins	Part A one compulsory task, Part B one chosen from four tasks offered (three general and one on set books) – two writing tasks in total
Paper 3	Use of English	1 hour 15 mins	five tasks – 65 questions
Paper 4	Listening	40 mins (approx.)	two longer recorded texts and two series of short extracts – 30 questions
Paper 5	Speaking	14 mins	An interaction between two candidates and an interlocutor/assessor. For assessment purposes a second assessor is present who takes no part in the interaction.

Special needs

Students who need special help or consideration, for example, the blind, deaf or otherwise physically disadvantaged, should contact UCLES at the address given, for information about the ways in which they can be helped to take the examination. UCLES will provide suitably modified papers and arrangements can be made for help at the time of the examination. Students with learning difficulties, for example dyslexia, may also receive special consideration if they can provide suitable documentation. Teachers should also be aware that it might be worth informing UCLES if students have had serious personal problems (such as bereavement) around the time of the exam.

Topics

The texts, speaking and writing exercises which form the basis of the First Certificate in English are drawn from a list of 25 broad topic areas. In preparing for the examination, it is advisable for students to aim to widen their vocabulary in as many of these areas as possible.

All 25 topics are represented in the eight tests which make up *Cambridge Practice Tests for First Certificate 1 & 2*. The list of specified topics is as follows:

- Personal life and circumstances e.g. personal experiences
- Living conditions e.g. where/how people live
- Occupations
- Education, study and learning
- Free-time activities
- Travel and tourism
- Consumer goods and shopping
- Eating and drinking
- Social/family relations
- The media
- The weather
- The environment/ecology
- Entertainment
- Health and exercise
- Services e.g. banks, post offices, etc.
- Places
- Language
- Music
- Fashion
- Animals
- Cinema
- History
- The Arts
- Sports
- People

A guide to the papers

Paper 1 Reading

Format

The Reading paper consists of four parts, each part containing one text (or a group of texts) along with a set of questions. **Part 1** is a multiple matching exercise (matching parts of the text to either relevant headings or summary sentences) with six or seven questions, **Part 2** is a multiple choice exercise with seven or eight questions, **Part 3** is a gapped-text exercise with six or seven questions (the gaps are either sentences or paragraphs) and **Part 4** is a multiple matching exercise (scanning a text to find specific information). The total number of questions on the paper is 35.

The tasks

The Reading paper aims to test a range of reading skills such as finding specific information and understanding gist, detail, the main idea, inference, cohesion, text structure, functional and sociolinguistic meaning. Students are encouraged to develop different reading skills in order to approach the different tasks in each part. Each task requires the employment of a range of skills but the main skill needed varies from one task to another, for example, **Part 1** requires reading for gist and detail, **Part 2** requires reading for detail and also for cohesion and global meaning, **Part 3** tests an understanding of text structure as well as reading for gist and detail and **Part 4** requires students to search for specific information. The position of the questions varies according to the nature of the task – for **Parts 1** and **4** the questions come first and for **Parts 2** and **4** the questions follow the text.

The texts

The texts come from a range of sources such as newspapers, magazines, books, brochures, leaflets and letters. These include articles, advertisements, reports, reviews, informational material, fiction and correspondence. One of the parts may contain a multi-text which consists of two or more shorter related texts. The aim is to present students with a range of real texts which they might come across in the English-speaking world. The texts are altered as little as possible but it is usually necessary to simplify some of the lexis as there are very few pieces in the real world which are written at FCE level. Texts may also be shortened. Illustrations may be used either as an aid to understanding an important concept or simply to retain the authenticity of the text. Where possible, the exam text will reflect the original in terms of layout and typeface.

    The length of the texts in each part varies but is in the range of 350–700 words per text with an overall total of 1900–2300 words over the whole paper.

At first glance, the number of words may seem daunting to a student, but not all the tasks require detailed reading. When preparing students for the Reading paper it is important to explain that it is not necessary for them to understand every single word of all the texts to answer the questions. Some of the lexis, which is neither central to the task nor necessary for an understanding of the whole text, is indeed above FCE level and can either be guessed or ignored.

Preparing students

If possible, students should be shown the different text types that appear in the exam, for example, newspapers, magazines, advertisements. If English Language publications are not available, students can be encouraged to look at local newspapers and magazines in their own language and talk about the different kinds of texts. Students can look at layouts and headlines and they should realise that they can get an idea of the nature of a text before they actually start to read. It is important that they become used to reading the instructions carefully as these explain not only what they have to do but also where the text came from, for example, a magazine article.

It is a good idea to explain to students that it is best to approach each part of the paper in a different way. If they read through every word of every text before looking at the questions, they are almost certain to run out of time. In **Parts 1** and **4** they should look at the questions first.

PART 1

The questions are either headings or summary sentences which should be matched to the relevant parts of the text. There is an example, which cannot be used again. The headings or summary sentences are jumbled. When students have read through the headings or sentences, they should then start reading the text. For each part of the text, they match the corresponding heading or sentence. If they are unsure of any, they should leave them until the end when there will be fewer to choose from. There is one extra heading or sentence which does not need to be used. When all the headings or sentences have been matched, students should go back and check as it is easy to miss something the first time. They should remember that there is only one heading or sentence that does not fit anywhere. Students can practise this type of task with real newspaper articles. Newspapers usually have short paragraphs summarising the day's news and each has a heading. They will probably be quite easy to match but it will give them valuable practice in skimming for gist and matching. Students could also try writing their own headings or summary sentences for articles or passages from a course book, then jumbling them up and giving them to other students to solve.

PART 2

Students can read the text first to get an overall understanding and then go back and look at it again in more detail while answering the multiple choice questions. There will probably be at least one question testing cohesion (e.g. 'What does *it* refer to in line 6?'). For this question, students need to practise looking around the word in the text and underlining the different choices. They should then read through that part of the text again, looking for clues which connect one of the options to 'it'. There will probably be a question which tests global understanding and students should be able to answer this once they have worked through the whole text.

PART 3

One sentence has been taken out of each paragraph, or every alternate paragraph has been removed. Students may find it easiest to read what is left of the original text to get an idea of what it is about and then look at the sentences or paragraphs which have been removed. There is one extra sentence or paragraph, which is not needed. The first gap is already completed as an example. Students should be encouraged to work through the text by reading the first paragraph and then finding which sentence or paragraph fits next. They can look for words which may help them such as pronouns, time indicators, sequencing of events, geographical locations. If they are unsure what fits in a gap, they should leave that one and continue. They can come back at the end and fill in the missing ones. If they fit the wrong paragraph or sentence into a gap near the beginning, it will then make the rest of the exercise very difficult. If there is time at the end, they could check around each gap to check it makes sense with what goes before and after. There will probably not be time to read through the whole text again.

As practice, the paragraphs of other texts could be cut up or sentences deleted. At first, the task could be attempted on texts which are already familiar to students. Help them to recognise the kind of words and phrases which link paragraphs and to look out for tense changes.

PART 4

The questions come before the text and are not in the same order as the information in the text. They ask students to look for specific information. Students should be encouraged to scan the text until they find the part which is relevant. They should then slow down and read in more detail. Each part of the text can be used more than once so the same number of choices stays in play throughout the task. Students need to learn to read these texts fairly quickly and not worry about individual words which they do not understand. The skill of retrieving specific information is one we use every day when looking for a telephone number, finding out what is on television, deciding which film to go and watch from a list of reviews, etc. Students need to realise that they carry out this kind of task every day in their own language and, if possible, they should practise some real-life task in English in class. It doesn't matter if the language is too difficult for them as long as the task is within their reach – it will train them to scan text for the relevant information.

Paper 2 Writing

Format

The Writing paper lasts one hour thirty minutes and is divided into two parts. **Part 1** consists of a compulsory letter. In **Part 2**, students choose one of five tasks. The word limit is 120–180 words for each part. Students write their answers in the question paper booklet.

The tasks

In **Part 1**, students are presented with a task by means of up to three short pieces of text such as advertisements, letters, notes, leaflets, diaries, timetables or notices. They are required to write a transactional letter, i.e. one that aims to achieve a given purpose. The purpose will vary according to context, for example, they may need to impart or request information, to describe or narrate, to complain or explain, and so on. The style will be neutral or slightly formal. The addressee and the purpose of the task will always be clearly stated in the rubric. In **Part 2**, students are offered five options which will always include: at least one situationally-based task such as a letter, report or application; at least one composition of a discursive, descriptive or narrative type; two alternative tasks on the prescribed background texts (see note on *set books* below). Students are expected to produce content and style appropriate to the given reader and purpose. **Part 1** also requires students to assimilate and select from the stimulus material. This part of the paper is designed to assist in the standardisation of marking as the task is common to all students. In any single test, the tasks in **Part 2** are designed to avoid duplication of the one in **Part 1**, so students must expect to write two quite different pieces.

Preparing students

The writing skills required for the two parts of this paper are broadly the same: the ability to write generally correct (but not flawless) straightforward English which demonstrates awareness of purpose and of the target reader in terms of both content and style.

In **Part 1**, it is particularly important for students to make intelligent use of the stimulus material. They should be trained to select and re-phrase appropriately and to avoid indiscriminate lifting. As well as practising a variety of writing tasks of the correct length and under examination conditions, it is also worth students' while to measure the extent of their handwriting when preparing for the examination, so that they can judge the length of their answers without wasting valuable time counting words during the examination itself.

For both **Parts 1** and **2**, it is a good idea to train students to analyse each task by means of the questions: *What* am I writing? (letter, report, story, etc.) *Who* am I writing for? (my teacher, a possible employer, other students, etc.) *Why* am I writing? (to inform, to entertain, to complain, etc.) and to understand the implications of their answers to these questions in terms of content and style. Use of underlining or a highlighter pen is recommended at this stage. They should then ask themselves: What shall I say? and be encouraged to make a brief plan of the content of their answer before beginning to write. This will allow them to concentrate on the quality of their language as they write, rather than being distracted by the search for ideas. In **Part 2**, it will also enable them to discover, before they have wasted too much time, if they have chosen a subject which they cannot handle confidently.

Set books

Students may choose to study one or more from a list of set books and answer a question on them in **Paper 2 Part 2**. Apart from any broader interest that students and teachers may have in studying these books, the main advantage as far as the examination is concerned lies in the fact that it enables students to write about subject matter with which they are thoroughly familiar. The books are either very straightforward original texts or simplified readers of an appropriate level. Literary criticism is not expected of candidates, but the tasks are likely to involve a range of language skills. For example, they may be asked to narrate a part of the story, describe a location or person, comment on actions or motives, or give their opinion about events or behaviour. The list of set books is published by UCLES in the examination regulations and the set books are changed every two years.

Paper 3 Use of English

Format

The Use of English paper consists of five parts. **Parts 1, 2, 4** and **5** each consist of a set of questions based on a short text. **Part 3** consists of ten separate questions. **Part 1** (15 questions) is a multiple-choice cloze exercise in which students choose the correct word(s) from four options to fill gaps in a text of around 200 words. **Part 2** (15 questions) is an 'open' cloze exercise which requires students to supply their own words (one word per gap) to complete a text of around 200 words. In **Part 3** (10 questions), students must complete a gap in a sentence (between two and five words per gap) so that it means the same as the sentence printed above it. They are given one 'key' word which must form part of the answer, and which must not be altered in any way. **Part 4** (15 questions) is an error-identification exercise. Students must identify correct and incorrect lines in a text of around 200 words. For incorrect lines, the extra *and unnecessary* word causing the error must also be identified. **Part 5** (10 questions) is a word-formation exercise. Students are required to fill gaps in a text of around 150 words by creating suitable parts of speech from the root words given. This may involve, for example, forming a noun from a verb (e.g. *appear → appearance*), an adverb from an adjective (e.g. *fortunate → unfortunately*), etc.

One hour fifteen minutes is allowed for the paper, which has a total of 65 questions. Answers are recorded on a separate answer sheet.

The tasks

The paper aims to test the student's knowledge of the lexical and grammatical systems of the language by means of questions which variously require the student to identify, select or supply appropriate responses. Each of the four text-based tasks requires the student to form a general idea of the context in order to appreciate fully the requirements of the individual questions. In **Part 3**, each of the discrete-sentence pairs can be viewed as a 'mini-text' performing a similar function.

Part 1 consists mainly of lexical questions focusing on the selection of the only option with the correct meaning for the context. A small proportion of the questions will also have a grammatical element, in that two or more options may have an appropriate meaning, and the final choice will rest on the grammatical compatibility of the options with the gap in question.

The 'open' gaps in **Part 2** are designed to focus mainly on structural elements of the language. Some items will have a clear lexical element (e.g. when the correct tense of a suitable verb must be supplied), but all words required will be well within the competence of the average FCE candidate.

Part 3 combines lexical and structural elements and samples the student's ability to produce longer sequences of language to complete the expression of a given meaning in a given way. By limiting the number of successful variations for any particular gap, the key word and the word limit enable a wide range of structural points to be tested reliably.

Part 4 tests the student's ability to identify a variety of errors in a piece of connected prose. The form of the error is always that of an *extra and unnecessary word*, but a wide variety of common errors can be tested in this way.

Part 5 tests the student's ability to identify the part of speech required to fill a gap in a text and to form the correct response from a given root word. The exact form of word required may be influenced by the wider context of the piece. This may mean, for example, that a negative adjective is required, rather than a positive one.

The texts

The texts for **Paper 3** are primarily a vehicle for the testing points they contain. They offer a certain amount of intrinsic interest, but operate at a lexical and conceptual level somewhat below the texts on the Reading paper, and are not intended to pose genuine comprehension problems for competent FCE candidates.

The texts for **Parts 1, 2** and **5** generally come from original sources such as newspapers, books and magazines. They are drawn from a range of text-types including factual, narrative, descriptive, discursive, imaginative, etc., and may be based on reports, articles, fiction, correspondence, informational material and so on. Because of the strict technical and lexical requirements of the examination, it is rarely possible to use original texts without a certain amount of editing and adaptation.

The text for **Part 4** is different, in that it is intended to represent a standard of English within the competence of the best FCE students. The texts are specially composed to reflect a broad spectrum of student error, since using a single authentic source would inevitably bias the test against students who shared the original writer's first language.

Preparing students

The total reading load of the paper is in the region of 1100 words. Slower readers can be put at a disadvantage, and so, as with the Reading paper, reading speed in English is worthy of attention in preparing for the examination. Practice in reading quickly for gist is particularly helpful.

With all text-based questions, it is advisable to read quickly through the text
first to form an overall impression of the context before attempting to mark any
answers. Students should not neglect the 'example' sentences at the beginning,
which may contain important contextual clues.

Great care should be taken with spelling throughout the paper.

Parts 1, 2, 3 and 5 are all gap-filling exercises and have certain technical
points in common, which can usefully be pointed out to students.

- The majority of structural and contextual clues to the correct answer will be
  found in the areas immediately before **or after** the gap. All students look
  before the gap. Incorrect answers, however, often demonstrate the failure to
  recognise the need for structural or lexical cohesion with what **follows** the
  gap.
- 'Problem' gaps in texts may be better passed over until most of the more
  straightforward answers have been made. As the text nears completion, it
  may be easier to deal with the more difficult items.
- Students should try to leave time to read quickly through the completed text
  to ensure that the whole piece makes sense.

SPECIFIC POINTS

Part 1   Correct answers must have the correct meaning for the context and
must fit successfully into the structure of the sentence. They may also have to
form part of a collocation or other fixed phrase.

In addition to general vocabulary work, it is advantageous for FCE students
to pay attention to collocations and other semantic sets as they occur in their
reading and classwork.

Part 2   All the missing words are essential to the structure of the sentence from
which they have been removed. Gaps can generally only be filled by one part of
speech. Some gaps may have alternative answers, but these will usually be near-
synonyms (e.g. *each/every; because/as/since*). Students should try to avoid
wasting time choosing the best of two or three equally correct responses.

Early practice can usefully concentrate on identifying the missing part of
speech. Students can gain confidence with the mechanics of the exercise by
producing their own short cloze tests.

Part 3   The correct answer should preserve all important elements of the
meaning from the original sentence. Students should not make unnecessary
changes in vocabulary. Otherwise correct answers which alter the key word in
any way or use too many words will be penalised.

Students should develop an awareness of points commonly tested, so that
they have an idea of what to look out for. Grammar work should take account
of the need at this level to be able to express the same idea in different ways, and
to move freely from one form to another.

Part 4   Of the fifteen lines tested, between three and five will be correct. The
extra words which must be identified are always clearly inappropriate, not just
optional additions, and may appear anywhere in the line: this means that a
word early in the line may be shown to be wrong because of something in the
previous line; a word near the end may be wrong because of the continuation on
the next line. For this reason, it is important to remind students that they are
dealing with **a complete text**, and not fifteen separate questions.

Students should be encouraged to check their own and/or colleagues' work whenever possible. Although the form of the errors they find will not always be the same as the FCE exercise (i.e. an extra word) many of the same structural points will be tested in the examination. The improvement of self-checking is obviously of great benefit to the Writing paper as well.

Part 5 No correct answer will involve making more than two changes to the original word given (e.g. *interest → uninterested* can be included, *interest → uninterestedly* cannot). Students should remain aware of the wider context for their answers: whether a person in a text is *fortunate* or *unfortunate* may depend on elements of the text which are some distance from the gap in question.

Students should be encouraged to develop an interest in word groups, and should receive guidance on extending their use of the dictionary and modifying their own strategy for recording new vocabulary if necessary. Common word groups can be usefully and enjoyably revised in a quiz format.

Paper 4 Listening

Format

The Listening paper is presented on audio cassette. Students can write on their question papers as they listen. The Paper lasts up to 45 minutes. This includes five minutes at the end when students copy their answers onto the answer sheet (see note on p. 33). There are four parts to each test and the structure of the test is always the same.

The tasks

Part 1 consists of eight three-option multiple choice questions, each of which is based on a different monologue or conversation about 30 seconds long. Students hear each monologue or conversation twice. The question and options are read out on the tape as well as being printed in the question paper, so students are in no danger of losing their place. **Part 2** consists of a monologue or conversation, about three minutes long, with ten note-taking, sentence-completion or open-question items. Students are given time to read through the questions before the piece begins. The entire piece is repeated. Students are not penalised for minor spelling errors, providing their answers are recognisable as correct. **Part 3** consists of five short monologues or conversations, each about 30 seconds in length. There is a list of six possible answers which students must match against the pieces they hear. The group of five pieces is repeated. **Part 4** is usually a conversation, about three minutes in length. There are seven items, which may be three-option multiple choice or some other objectively marked type, such as True/False. They will not be note-taking items. There is time to read the items through before listening and the entire piece is repeated.

The Listening paper aims to test a range of skills, such as listening for gist and identifying the speaker, attitude or purpose. The format of **Part 1** allows students to have several 'fresh starts' so that they are less likely to feel discouraged in the early stages of the test. The fixed structure of the test is also designed to make students feel more secure in what is generally considered to be the most stressful part of the examination.

Preparing students

The best preparation for the Listening paper is exposure to a wide variety of spoken English. Students should be encouraged to listen to English in any form available, both in school and outside. For students who are not in an English-speaking country, information about English language broadcasts on the radio or television should be made available and students should be encouraged to seek out and share recorded material such as audio cassettes of pop songs and videos of films in English. It is not necessary for such material to use standard UK English. The important thing is for students to become habituated to listening to spoken English without a preamble in their mother tongue. In any case, some of the accents in the FCE examination are not standard UK, although they will never be very strong.

It is also essential for students to become thoroughly familiar with the format and aims of the Listening paper and to understand what is required in the different stages of the test. It is a good idea to introduce the Listening paper gradually by using one of the tests in this book simply to demonstrate what is required.

Students should also learn to use the printed questions as clues to what they will hear. Group discussion before listening will help to develop this skill. Teachers should bear in mind that these Practice Tests are at the level of difficulty of the examination and care should be taken not to undermine students' confidence by exposing them to the listening tasks under examination conditions too early.

Paper 5 Speaking

Format

The Speaking paper is designed to produce a sample of language from students which demonstrates their ability to give and exchange information and opinions. It lasts 14 minutes and is divided into four parts in order to draw out different types of language.

Students are examined in pairs, allowing for a wide range of speaking skills to be sampled. There are also two examiners: an interlocutor, who conducts the test and contributes to assessment, and an assessor, who takes no part in the conversation, and is therefore free to concentrate entirely on assessing the students according to the FCE criteria.

The two examiners may exchange roles during the course of an examining session, but not during the examining of any one pair of students.

Note: The two candidates / two examiners interview format applies in almost all cases. Only in very exceptional circumstances may a small number of centres vary this by special arrangement with UCLES.

The tasks

The Speaking paper aims to sample a wide range of language, from simple social interaction to the more sophisticated exchanges required to solve problems, reach agreement or agree to differ, etc. Students should be encouraged to gain as much practical speaking experience as possible in order to build up their confidence in dealing with each part of the test. Each task requires the employment of a range of skills, and involves a slightly different type of interaction.

Part 1 (three minutes) provides an opportunity for the two students to become accustomed to the examiners, each other and the examination situation while talking about familiar topics such as their personal background, interests, etc. Each student has a separate turn. This part of the paper tests mainly social language.

In **Part 2** (four minutes), each student in turn is given two colour photos and is invited to talk about the photos and the related theme. Comments may be general or may relate to the student her/himself if appropriate. Some mention of the content of the photos will be appropriate, but this part should **not** be treated as an exercise in close description. This part of the paper tests the ability to convey information and express opinions.

In **Part 3** (three minutes), the interlocutor gives the two students a visual stimulus (map, advertisements, photographs, etc.), which forms the basis of a joint task (prioritising, planning, decision-making, problem-solving, etc.). This task is on a different theme from **Part 2**. The students work on the task together, with the interlocutor offering only occasional guidance if required. This part of the paper requires the ability to negotiate and collaborate successfully in English, and tests the ability to exchange information and opinion, in conjunction with turn-taking and conversation management.

Part 4 (four minutes), is an extension of **Part 3**, in which the students are invited by the interlocutor to discuss ideas related to the theme of **Part 3**. The interlocutor asks questions to facilitate a fruitful discussion. This part of the paper is an opportunity to extend and develop ideas from **Part 3** in a wider context, and tests the ability to formulate opinions and respond appropriately to those of the other student. Turn-taking again plays an important part.

Preparing students

PAIRWORK

Because the Speaking paper is conducted with pairs of students, it is normally relatively easy to incorporate examination practice into class activities.

For practical or pedagogical reasons, however, students in some learning situations may be unfamiliar with pairwork. In such cases, paired practice becomes particularly important, since students in this position, while quite happy to respond to their teacher in English, may find using the language to converse with their classmates artificial or even embarrassing. Such feelings are not conducive to making a good impression in the examination room. Equally, turn-taking and collaborative conversation are important features of the

Speaking paper. Students should practise these skills with each other, as they may not find it easy to question, interrupt or disagree with their teacher, even for the sake of practice.

If possible, it is also well worth working occasionally in threes or fours, with one student, or pair of students, acting as the examiner(s). Observing a pair in action, and having to manage the timing and the various tasks, can give a useful insight into what is expected in the examination.

GENERAL POINTS

The material for Paper 5 Part 2 in this book is organised thematically to facilitate concerted vocabulary and practice in the preparatory stages. The FCE examination itself may not have a thematic link in Part 2. Teachers who wish to reproduce full examination conditions in the later stages of their course, or for mock examination purposes, should simply combine the material from Tests 3 and 4 as follows:

For Test 3, use	3A and 3B with 4C and 4D	for Part 2;
	3E	for Part 3
For Test 4, use	4A and 4B with 3C and 3D	for Part 2;
	4E	for Part 3

Students should be encouraged to view the Speaking paper as an opportunity to demonstrate their ability, rather than a threat. The visual material is chosen to provide starting points for the development of productive exchanges between the participants, and not to catch students out on particular points of vocabulary or grammar. Tasks can, however, range across the 25 broad topic areas listed on page 3, and it is advisable for students to equip themselves with sufficient vocabulary to take part in a general conversation on any of these.

The practical side of taking part in the examination should not be neglected. A significant proportion of what a student says in the examination room is not governed by the themes of **Parts 2, 3** and **4**. Study, and regular practice, of the language required to introduce oneself, meet new people, express opinions, make suggestions, take turns, disagree politely, make a composed apology for errors, etc. will all help students to establish the core of a creditable performance. Students may need convincing, but skills like these are the real focus of the test, not the photographs and other material which serve as a vehicle for the Paper.

It is also useful to do some work on locating particular elements within the frame of a picture (*the man on the left, the house in the top left-hand corner*) or in relation to other elements in the picture (*the taller of the two women, the house opposite the cinema*). Pointing things out physically should be avoided.

It may be important to emphasise to some students that an item-by-item description of a photograph is not required by any of the tasks, and that such a description at this level is likely to be simple and repetitive in structure. It will also leave few openings for further discussion, a significant element in **Parts 2** and **4**, and for these reasons, it is unlikely to generate a good score on the Paper.

Teachers may wish to co-ordinate Speaking and Writing preparation, since both require the development of topic vocabulary. Simple additions to classwork (e.g. putting students in pairs to tell each other what they have written in their homework compositions and discuss any points arising) can be of tremendous benefit in mobilising recently acquired language. This type of activity should be kept short and to the point, and the importance of starting promptly should be emphasised. The timing of the Speaking paper is very tight, and it is important to avoid having thirty seconds' silence at the start of a three-minute task. Making students start quickly also encourages them to develop the skill of thinking 'on their feet' in English, which contributes greatly to taking a natural part in a fast-moving conversation.

Paper 5 frameworks

Book 1 Test 1

Note: The colour pictures needed for Paper 5 appear on pages C1–12 in Student's Book 1.

Part 1 (three minutes)

Introduce yourself and the assessor.*
Encourage each candidate in turn to give personal information using questions such as:
>   Where/What part of … are you from?
>   How long have you lived here/there?
>   Tell us what it's like living here/there …
If not in student's home town/country: What are the main differences between here and your home town/country?

Part 2 (four minutes)

Tell the candidates what is going to happen:
>   Now I'd like each of you to talk on your own for about a minute.
Say something like:
>   I'm going to give each of you two different pictures and I'd like you to talk about them and say whether you'd like to study in this sort of place.
>   (Candidate A), here are your two pictures. Please let (Candidate B) see them. They show different places where you might study.
Indicate the pictures 1A and 1B to Candidate A. Say:
>   (Candidate B), I'll give you your two pictures in a moment.
Then invite Candidate A to begin, by saying, for example:
>   (Candidate A), I'd like you to compare and contrast these pictures, saying how you'd feel about studying in such places. Remember, you have only about a minute for this, so don't worry if I interrupt you. All right?
Candidate A speaks for approximately one minute.
Thank Candidate A, retrieve the pictures and invite Candidate B to speak:
>   (Candidate B), could you tell us which of those places you would prefer to study in?
Candidate B speaks for approximately 20 seconds.
>   Thank you. Now, (Candidate B), here are your pictures. Please let (Candidate A) see them. They show some other places to study.

---

* The assessor may not of course be present when students are practising with their teacher, but they should become accustomed to the idea that there will be a second examiner in the room who does not join in their conversation (see p. 12).

Indicate the pictures 1C and 1D to Candidate B. Say something like:
> (Candidate B), I'd like you to compare and contrast these study environments and say whether you prefer one of them. Do you ever study in places like these? Remember, you have only about a minute for this, so don't worry if I interrupt you. All right?

Candidate B speaks for approximately one minute.
Thank Candidate B.
Retrieve the pictures and say something like:
> (Candidate A), could you tell us which of those places you'd prefer to study in?

Candidate A speaks for approximately 20 seconds.
Thank the candidates and move on to Part 3.

Part 3 (three minutes)

Say:
> Now, I'd like you to do something together.

Indicate the town plan (1E) to both candidates. Ask them to consider which of the three locations A, B, or C would be the best site for a new hospital. Say:
> Here is a plan of part of a town. You can see three areas marked A, B and C. The town is going to have a new hospital. I'd like you to talk together and decide which of the areas marked would be best and why. It is not necessary to agree with each other. All right? You have only about three minutes for this, so, once again, don't worry if I stop you and please speak so that we can hear you.

If the candidates are having difficulty keeping the conversation going, it may be necessary to support them with an extra question or remark, but it is important to avoid stepping in too soon.
After about three minutes thank the candidates and move on to Part 4.

Part 4 (four minutes)

Encourage the candidates to develop topics raised by their discussion in Part 3.
Depending on the way their discussion went, possible questions might be:
> Are cities too noisy?
> What can be done to reduce noise pollution in cities?

> How important is it that there should be good public transport?
> Do people use private cars too much? Why?
> Do you think the traffic in cities should be controlled more strictly? How?

> Is it important for local people to be involved in planning decisions? Why?
> Are local people sufficiently involved in planning decisions on the whole?
> If not, why not? What could be done to improve this?

Book 1 Test 2

Note: The colour pictures needed for Paper 5 appear on pages C1–12 in Student's Book 1.

Part 1 *(three minutes)*

Introduce yourself and the assessor.*
Encourage each candidate in turn to give personal information using questions such as:

Do you have brothers and sisters? Tell me something about them ...

Do you get on well together?

What are the advantages/disadvantages of being an only child/a member of a large family?

Do you see much of the older members of your family? Your grandparents, for example?

Part 2 *(four minutes)*

Tell the candidates what is going to happen:

Now I'd like each of you to talk on your own for about a minute.

Say something like:

I'm going to give each of you two different pictures and I'd like you to talk about them and say whether you like to eat in this sort of place.

(Candidate A), here are your two pictures. Please let (Candidate B) see them. They show different places where you might eat.

Indicate the pictures 2A and 2B to Candidate A. Say:

(Candidate B), I'll give you your two pictures in a moment.

Then invite Candidate A to begin, by saying, for example:

(Candidate A), I'd like you to compare and contrast these pictures, saying how you'd feel about eating in such places. Remember, you have only about a minute for this, so don't worry if I interrupt you. All right?

Candidate A speaks for approximately one minute.

Thank Candidate A, retrieve the pictures and invite Candidate B to speak:

(Candidate B), could you tell us which of those places you would prefer to eat in?

Candidate B speaks for approximately 20 seconds.

Thank you. Now, (Candidate B), here are your pictures. Please let (Candidate A) see them. They show some other places to eat.

Indicate the pictures 2C and 2D to Candidate B. Say something like:

(Candidate B), I'd like you to compare and contrast these places and say whether you prefer one of them? Do you ever eat in places like these? Remember, you have only about a minute for this, so don't worry if I interrupt you. All right?

Candidate B speaks for approximately one minute.

---

* The assessor may not of course be present when students are practising with their teacher, but they should become accustomed to the idea that there will be a second examiner in the room who does not join in their conversation (see p. 12).

Thank Candidate B.
Retrieve the pictures and say something like:
   (Candidate A), could you tell us which of these places you'd prefer to eat in?
Candidate A speaks for approximately 20 seconds.
Thank the candidates and move on to Part 3.

Part 3 (three minutes)

Say:
   Now, I'd like you to do something together.
Indicate the presents (2E) and the pictures of people (2F) to both candidates.
Ask them to decide which of the presents would be most suitable for each of
their 'friends'. Say:
   Here are some presents you might buy in Britain to take to friends abroad.
   Here are four people you want to choose presents for. I'd like you to talk
   together and decide which present would be best for each person and why. It
   is not necessary to agree with each other. All right? You have only about
   three minutes for this, so, once again, don't worry if I stop you and please
   speak so that we can hear you.
If the candidates are having difficulty keeping the conversation going, it may be
necessary to support them with an extra question or remark, but it is important
to avoid stepping in too soon.
After about three minutes thank the candidates and move on to Part 4.

Part 4 (four minutes)

Encourage the candidates to develop topics raised by their discussion in Part 3.
Depending on the way their discussion went, possible questions might be:
   Do you enjoy giving people presents? Why/Why not?
   How do you decide what to give?

   When do people give presents in your country?
   For birthdays, special occasions …?
   What sort of things do they give?
   Are there any traditions in your country about giving or receiving presents?
   For example, should you open a present immediately when you are given it?
   Why/Why not?

   Do people spend too much money on unnecessary things nowadays, things
   like tourist souvenirs …?

   What sort of things do people buy as souvenirs from your country?
   Do you think these are the right sort of things for them to buy?

Book 1 Test 3

Note: The colour pictures needed for Paper 5 appear on pages C1–12 in Student's Book 1.

Part 1 *(three minutes)*

Introduce yourself and the assessor.*
Encourage each candidate in turn to give personal information using questions such as:
> What do you enjoy doing in your free time?
> Tell me a bit about what you actually do when you …
> How long have you been interested in …?
> Can you explain something about the rules of …/why people enjoy …/the attraction of …?

Part 2 *(four minutes)*

Tell the candidates what is going to happen:
> Now I'd like each of you to talk on your own for about a minute.
Say something like:
> I'm going to give each of you two different pictures and I'd like you to talk about them and say whether you'd like to travel this way.
> (Candidate A), here are your two pictures. Please let (Candidate B) see them. They show different ways of travelling.
Indicate the pictures 3A and 3B to Candidate A. Say:
> (Candidate B), I'll give you your two pictures in a moment.
Then invite Candidate A to begin, by saying, for example:
> (Candidate A), I'd like you to compare and contrast these pictures, saying how you'd feel about travelling like this. Remember, you have only about a minute for this, so don't worry if I interrupt you. All right?
Candidate A speaks for approximately one minute.
Thank Candidate A, retrieve the pictures and invite Candidate B to speak:
> (Candidate B), could you tell us which of those ways of travelling you would prefer?
Candidate B speaks for approximately 20 seconds.
> Thank you. Now, (Candidate B), here are your pictures. Please let (Candidate A) see them. They show some other ways of travelling.
Indicate the pictures 3C and 3D to Candidate B. Say something like:
> (Candidate B), I'd like you to compare and contrast these ways of travelling and say whether you prefer one of them. Have you ever travelled like this? Remember, you have only about a minute for this, so don't worry if I interrupt you. All right?
Candidate B speaks for approximately one minute.
Thank Candidate B.

---

* The assessor may not of course be present when students are practising with their teacher, but they should become accustomed to the idea that there will be a second examiner in the room who does not join in their conversation (see p. 12).

Retrieve the pictures and say something like:
    (Candidate A), could you tell us which of those ways you'd prefer to travel?
Candidate A speaks for approximately 20 seconds.
Thank the candidates and move on to Part 3.

Part 3 (three minutes)

Say:
    Now, I'd like you to do something together.
Indicate the illustration 'Success in Sport' (3E) to both candidates. Ask them to consider which of the reasons given are most important in deciding whether people are successful in sport. Say:
    Here are some reasons why people succeed in sport. I'd like you to talk together and decide which are the most important and which don't matter so much. It is not necessary to agree with each other. All right? You have only about three minutes for this, so, once again, don't worry if I stop you and please speak so that we can hear you.
If the candidates are having difficulty keeping the conversation going, it may be necessary to support them with an extra question or remark, but it is important to avoid stepping in too soon.
After about three minutes thank the candidates and move on to Part 4.

Part 4 (four minutes)

Encourage the candidates to develop topics raised by their discussion in Part 3.
Depending on the way their discussion went, possible questions might be:
    Is it better to watch sport on television or live?
    Are famous sports people good models for young people to follow?
    Why/Why not?
    What dangers are involved in international sport?
    Is there too much advertising in sport?
    Do people attach too much importance to sports nowadays? Why/Why not?

    What could be done to help young sportsmen and women in your area?
    Should governments give more support to young sportsmen and women?
    Why/Why not?

Book 1 Test 4

Note: The colour pictures needed for Paper 5 appear on pages C1–12 in Student's Book 1.

Part 1 (three minutes)

Introduce yourself and the assessor.*
Encourage each candidate in turn to give personal information using questions such as:

Are you studying English for any special purpose?
In what way do you think English will be useful to you in the future?
If not, why not?
What other languages do you/would you like to study? Why?
Can you tell me about your career plans?

For candidates still at school: What will you do when you leave school?

Part 2 (four minutes)

Tell the candidates what is going to happen:

Now I'd like each of you to talk on your own for about a minute.

Say something like:

I'm going to give each of you two different pictures of houses and I'd like you to talk about them and say what you think it would be like to live in these places.
(Candidate A), here are your two pictures. Please let (Candidate B) see them. They show different houses.

Indicate the pictures 4A and 4B to Candidate A. Say:

(Candidate B), I'll give you your two pictures in a moment.

Then invite Candidate A to begin, by saying, for example:

(Candidate A), I'd like you to compare and contrast these pictures, saying how you'd feel about living in such places. Remember, you only have about a minute for this, so don't worry if I interrupt you. All right?

Candidate A speaks for approximately one minute.
Thank Candidate A, retrieve the pictures and invite Candidate B to speak:

(Candidate B), could you tell us which of those places you would prefer to live in?

Candidate B speaks for approximately 20 seconds.

Thank you. Now, (Candidate B), here are your pictures. Please let (Candidate A) see them. They show some other houses.

Indicate the pictures 4C and 4D to Candidate B. Say something like:

(Candidate B), I'd like you to compare and contrast these houses and say whether you prefer one of them. Have you ever lived in places like these? Remember, you have only about a minute for this so don't worry if I interrupt you. All right?

---

* The assessor may not of course be present when students are practising with their teacher, but they should become accustomed to the idea that there will be a second examiner in the room who does not join in their conversation (see p. 12).

Candidate B speaks for approximately one minute.
Thank Candidate B.
Retrieve the pictures and say something like:
   (Candidate A), could you tell us which of those places you'd prefer to live in?
Candidate A speaks for approximately 20 seconds.
Thank the candidates and move on to Part 3.

Part 3 (three minutes)

Say:
   Now, I'd like you to do something together.
Indicate the photograph 4E to both candidates. Tell them that this is someone
who is going for a job interview and needs some advice. Ask them to discuss
what they should tell her. Say:
   Here is a young woman who wants to get a job looking after elderly people.
   She's going for her interview tomorrow and she wants your advice about her
   appearance. I'd like you to talk together and discuss whether she should
   change her appearance, and if so, how. It is not necessary to agree with each
   other. All right? You have only about three minutes for this, so, once again,
   don't worry if I stop you and please speak so that we can hear you.
If the candidates are having difficulty keeping the conversation going, it may be
necessary to support them with an extra question or remark, but it is important
to avoid stepping in too soon.
After about three minutes thank the candidates and move on to Part 4.

Part 4 (four minutes)

Encourage the candidates to develop topics raised by their discussion in Part 3.
Depending on the way their discussion went, possible questions might be:
   Do you think it's important to dress smartly for work?
   Have you ever had problems with your teachers or parents about the clothes
   you wear?
   Why do some young people wear very unusual clothes?
   Do people's clothes tell you about their personalities?
   How much do you care about being in fashion?
   Are fashion clothes good value for money?
   Do fashions have too much influence on what people buy?

Book 2 Test 1

Note: The colour pictures needed for Paper 5 appear on pages C1–12 in Student's Book 2.

Part 1 *(three minutes)*

Introduce yourself and the assessor.*
Encourage each candidate in turn to give personal information using questions such as:
    Where/What part of … are you from?
    How long have you lived here/there?
    Tell us what it's like living here/there …
If not in student's home town/country:
    What are the main differences between here and your home town/country?

Part 2 *(four minutes)*

Tell the candidates what is going to happen:
    Now I'd like each of you to talk on your own for about a minute.
Say something like:
    I'm going to give each of you two different pictures and I'd like you to talk about them and say whether you like them or not.
    (Candidate A), here are your two pictures. Please let (Candidate B) see them.
Indicate pictures 1A and 1B to Candidate A. Say:
    (Candidate B), I'll give you your two pictures in a moment.
Then invite Candidate A to begin, by saying, for example:
    (Candidate A), I'd like you to compare and contrast these pictures, saying what you like or dislike about them. Remember, you have only about a minute for this, so don't worry if I interrupt you. All right?
Candidate A speaks for approximately one minute.
Thank Candidate A, retrieve the pictures and invite Candidate B to speak:
    (Candidate B), could you tell us which of those pictures you prefer?
Candidate B speaks for approximately 20 seconds.
    Thank you. Now, (Candidate B), here are your pictures. Please let (Candidate A) see them.
Indicate pictures 1C and 1D to Candidate B. Say something like:
    (Candidate B), I'd like you to compare and contrast these pictures and say what you like or dislike about them. Would you like to have one of them in your house? Remember, you have only about a minute for this, so don't worry if I interrupt you. All right?
Candidate B speaks for approximately one minute.
Thank Candidate B.

---

* The assessor may not of course be present when students are practising with their teacher, but they should become accustomed to the idea that there will be a second examiner in the room who does not join in their conversation (see p. 12).

Retrieve the pictures and say something like:
    (Candidate A), could you tell us which of those pictures you prefer?
Candidate A speaks for approximately 20 seconds.
Thank the candidates and move on to Part 3.

Part 3 (three minutes)

Say:
    Now, I'd like you to do something together.
Indicate the plan of a youth centre (1E) to both candidates. Ask them to
consider how they would use the different rooms. Say:
    Here is a plan of a building which is going to be used as a youth centre. You
    can see the different rooms. I'd like you to talk together and decide how you
    would use the different rooms. For example, where would you put the toilets
    and the café? It is not necessary to agree with each other. All right? You have
    only about three minutes for this, so, once again, don't worry if I stop you
    and please speak so that we can hear you.
If the candidates are having difficulty keeping the conversation going, it may be
necessary to support them with an extra question or remark, but it is important
to avoid stepping in too soon.
After about three minutes thank the candidates and move on to Part 4.

Part 4 (four minutes)

Encourage the candidates to develop topics raised by their discussion in Part 3.
Depending on the way their discussion went, possible questions (depending on
the age of the candidates) might be:
    Have you ever been to a youth centre? / Did you use a youth centre when you
    were a teenager?
    Do you think it is important to have places where young people can meet?
    Why or why not?
    What kinds of activities should youth centres offer?
    How often should they be open and at what times of day?
    How should they be paid for?
    Do you think there are enough places for young people to go in their free
    time?
    Are young people offered too much entertainment nowadays? Does this
    mean they aren't used to amusing themselves?
    Do you think some crimes happen because young people haven't got enough
    to do? What can be done about this?

Book 2 Test 2

Note: The colour pictures needed for Paper 5 appear on pages C1–12 in Student's Book 2.

Part 1 *(three minutes)*

*Introduce yourself and the assessor.**
Encourage each candidate in turn to give personal information using questions such as:

Do you have brothers and sisters? Tell me something about them.

Do you get on well together?

What are the advantages/disadvantages of being an only child/member of a large family?

Do you see much of the older members of your family? Your grandparents, for example?

Part 2 *(four minutes)*

Tell the candidates what is going to happen:

Now I'd like each of you to talk on your own for about a minute.

Say something like:

I'm going to give each of you two different pictures of places where you might go to find clothes and I'd like you to talk about them and say whether you might go to them or not.

(Candidate A), here are your two pictures. Please let (Candidate B) see them. They show different places where you might go to find clothes.

Indicate pictures 2A and 2B to Candidate A. Say:

(Candidate B), I'll give you your two pictures in a moment.

Then invite Candidate A to begin, by saying, for example:

(Candidate A), I'd like you to compare and contrast the places shown in these pictures and say whether you would choose to go there to get ideas about what to wear. Remember, you have only about a minute for this, so don't worry if I interrupt you. All right?

Candidate A speaks for approximately one minute.

Thank Candidate A, retrieve the pictures and invite Candidate B to speak:

(Candidate B), could you tell us which of those places you prefer?

Candidate B speaks for approximately 20 seconds.

Thank you. Now, (Candidate B), here are your pictures. Please let (Candidate A) see them. They show some other places where you might go to find something to wear.

Indicate pictures 2C and 2D to Candidate B. Say something like:

(Candidate B), I'd like you to compare and contrast these places and say whether you would buy clothes there. Remember, you have only about a minute for this, so don't worry if I interrupt you. All right?

---

* The assessor may not of course be present when students are practising with their teacher, but they should become accustomed to the idea that there will be a second examiner in the room who does not join in their conversation (see p. 12).

Candidate B speaks for approximately one minute.
Thank Candidate B.
Retrieve the pictures and say something like:
  (Candidate A), could you tell us which of these places you prefer?
Candidate A speaks for approximately 20 seconds.
Thank the candidates and move on to Part 3.

Part 3 (three minutes)

Say:
  Now, I'd like you to do something together.
Indicate to both candidates the pictures of items (2E) that a student might want
to have in a study bedroom. Ask them to consider which items they would
choose. Say:
  Now, (Candidate A) and (Candidate B), you are each moving into a study
  bedroom. I'd like you to talk together and decide which of these items you
  would choose to have in your room. Say why you have chosen them. It is not
  necessary to agree with each other. All right? You only have three minutes for
  this, so, once again, don't worry if I stop you and please speak so that we can
  hear you.
If the candidates are having difficulty keeping the conversation going, it may be
necessary to support them with an extra question or remark, but it is important
to avoid stepping in too soon.
After about three minutes thank the candidates and move on to Part 4.

Part 4 (four minutes)

Encourage the candidates to develop topics raised by their discussion in Part 3.
Depending on the way their discussion went, possible questions might be:
  Are there any other things you would want in a room of your own?
  Are your possessions important to you? What kinds of things are most
  important?
  Do you think it is important for people to have a room of their own to study
  in?
  Are you a tidy person? How important is it to you to a keep a room tidy?
  Have you ever shared a room or an office with anyone? How did you get on?
  Were there any problems?

Book 2 Test 3

Note: The colour pictures needed for Paper 5 appear on pages C1–12 in Student's Book 2.

Part 1 (three minutes)

Introduce yourself and the assessor.*
Encourage each candidate in turn to give personal information using questions such as:
>   What do you enjoy doing in your free time?
>   Tell me a bit about what you actually do when you ...
>   How long have you been interested in ...?
>   Can you explain something about the rules of ... / why people enjoy ... / the attraction of ...?

Part 2 (four minutes)

Tell the candidates what is going to happen:
>   Now I'd like each of you to talk on your own for about a minute.

Say something like:
>   I'm going to give each of you two pictures of people doing different sports and I'd like you to talk about them and say whether you think these sports are enjoyable or not.
>   (Candidate A), here are your two pictures. Please let (Candidate B) see them. They show people doing different sports.

Indicate pictures 3A and 3B to Candidate A. Say:
>   (Candidate B), I'll give you your two pictures in a moment.

Then invite Candidate A to begin, by saying, for example:
>   (Candidate A), I'd like you to compare and contrast the sports shown in your pictures and say whether you ever do them or would like to do them. You have about one minute for this, so don't worry if I interrupt you. All right?

Candidate A speaks for approximately one minute.

Thank Candidate A, retrieve the pictures and invite Candidate B to speak:
>   (Candidate B), could you tell us which of those sports you think would be most enjoyable?

Candidate B speaks for approximately 20 seconds.
>   Thank you. Now, (Candidate B), here are your pictures. Please let (Candidate A) see them. They show some other sports.

Indicate pictures 3C and 3D to Candidate B. Say something like:
>   (Candidate B), I'd like you to compare and contrast these sports. Have you ever done anything like this or would you like to? Remember, you have only about a minute for this, so don't worry if I interrupt you. All right?

Candidate B speaks for approximately one minute.
Thank Candidate B.

---

* The assessor may not of course be present when students are practising with their teacher, but they should become accustomed to the idea that there will be a second examiner in the room who does not join in their conversation (see p. 12).

Retrieve the pictures and say something like:
    (Candidate A), could you tell us which of those sports you prefer?
Candidate A speaks for approximately 20 seconds.
Thank the candidates and move on to Part 3.

Part 3 (three minutes)

Say:
    Now, I'd like you to do something together.
Indicate to both candidates the illustrations showing the different ways of
improving the environment (3E) and ask the candidates to discuss them. Say:
    Here are some different ways that we can improve or protect the
    environment. I'd like you to talk together and decide which method is best for
    the environment. Think also about the cost involved. It is not necessary to
    agree with each other. All right? You only have three minutes for this, so, once
    again, don't worry if I stop you and please speak so that we can hear you.
If the candidates are having difficulty keeping the conversation going, it may be
necessary to support them with an extra question or remark, but it is important
to avoid stepping in too soon.
After about three minutes thank the candidates and move on to Part 4.

Part 4 (four minutes)

Encourage the candidates to develop topics raised by their discussion in Part 3.
Depending on the way their discussion went, possible questions might be:
    Do you think enough money is spent on the environment?
    If you had some money to spend on an environmental project, how would
    you spend it?
    Are most people in your country interested in protecting the environment?
    Do you think they should be more aware?
    How can people be educated to care about the environment?
    Are there other problems which are more important than the environment
    that we should spend time and money on?

Book 2 Test 4

Note: The colour pictures needed for Paper 5 appear on pages C1–12 in Student's Book 2.

Part 1 *(three minutes)*

Introduce yourself and the assessor.*
Encourage each candidate in turn to give personal information using questions such as:

Are you studying English for any special purpose?
In what way do you think English will be useful to you in the future?
If not, why not?
What other languages do you/would you like to study? Why?
Can you tell me about your career plans?
(If they are still at school) What will you do when you leave school?

Part 2 *(four minutes)*

Tell the candidates what is going to happen:
Now I'd like each of you to talk on your own for about a minute.
Say something like:
I'm going to give each of you two pictures of people performing different kinds of music. I'd like you to talk about your pictures and say whether you think you'd like to go and hear that kind of music.
(Candidate A), here are your two pictures. Please let (Candidate B) see them. They show people performing music.
Indicate pictures 4A and 4B to Candidate A. Say:
(Candidate B), I'll give you your two pictures in a moment.
Then invite Candidate A to begin, by saying, for example:
(Candidate A), I'd like you to compare and contrast these pictures and talk about the kinds of music you think the people are performing. Say whether you'd like to listen to it or not. Remember, you only have about a minute for this, so don't worry if I interrupt you. All right?
Candidate A speaks for approximately one minute.
Thank Candidate A, retrieve the pictures and invite Candidate B to speak:
(Candidate B), could you tell us which of those sorts of music you prefer?
Candidate B speaks for approximately 20 seconds.
Thank you. Now, (Candidate B), here are your pictures. Please let (Candidate A) see them. They show other performers.
Indicate pictures 4C and 4D to Candidate B. Say something like:
(Candidate B), I'd like you to compare and contrast these pictures of people performing different kinds of music and say whether you'd like to listen to it or not. Remember, you have only about a minute for this so don't worry if I interrupt you. All right?

---

* The assessor may not of course be present when students are practising with their teacher, but they should become accustomed to the idea that there will be a second examiner in the room who does not join in their conversation (see p. 12).

Candidate B speaks for approximately one minute.
Thank Candidate B.
Retrieve the pictures and say something like:
   (Candidate A), could you tell us which of those sorts of music you prefer?
Candidate A speaks for approximately 20 seconds.
Thank the candidates and move on to Part 3.

Part 3 *(three minutes)*

Say:
   Now, I'd like you to do something together.
Indicate to both candidates the illustrations (4E) which show the different ways
of campaigning to prevent a swimming-pool from closing down and ask
candidates to discuss them. Say:
   A swimming-pool is going to be closed and you want to keep it open. Here
   are some ways of getting support for your ideas. I'd like you to talk together
   and decide which method is likely to be most successful. It is not necessary to
   agree with each other. All right? You only have three minutes for this, so,
   once again, don't worry if I stop you, and please speak so that we can hear
   you.
If the candidates are having difficulty keeping the conversation going, it may be
necessary to support them with an extra question or remark, but it is important
to avoid stepping in too soon.
After about three minutes thank the candidates and move on to Part 4.

Part 4 *(four minutes)*

Encourage the candidates to develop topics raised by their discussion in Part 3.
Depending on the way their discussion went, possible questions might be:
   Have you ever tried to stop something happening? What did you do?
   Do you think people have enough control over what happens in the area they
   live in?
   Who makes decisions about this sort of thing?
   Is enough money spent on facilities like swimming-pools in your town?
   What sort of places for sport or entertainment would you like to see opened
   around where you live?

Recording answers

Paper 1, Paper 3 and Paper 4

Answers for these papers are recorded on computerised answer sheets which are marked by OMR (Optical Mark Reader). Samples are given in the Student's Book and these may be photocopied without further permission. Teachers are strongly advised to encourage the use of these sheets whenever possible, so that students are not troubled or distracted during the actual examination by the mechanics of recording their answers.

Paper 1

For this paper, students shade in lozenges in pencil to indicate their answers, A, B, C etc. These pencil marks are read by the OMR. It is important that students use soft pencil as the OMR is not sensitive to ink. If a mistake is made, students should carefully erase the mark with a rubber. Correcting fluid should not be used.

It is better for students to answer directly onto the OMR sheet rather than copy answers at the end to avoid making copying errors under pressure of time. Particular care should be taken not to record answers against the wrong question numbers, for example when leaving an answer blank. If any questions remain unanswered at the end, it is better to fill in a guess than to leave a blank.

Part 4 may include questions which require two or more answers. These may be given in any order.

Paper 3 and Paper 4

Although these papers are marked by hand, OMR sheets are used to speed up processing and ensure accuracy of addition. Some parts (Paper 3 Part 1, Paper 4 Parts 1 and 3) require students to shade in lozenges in pencil, as for Paper 1. The other parts require students to write in an answer. For these, students should write clearly, preferably in ink, in the spaces provided. Errors with shaded lozenges should be carefully erased, as for Paper 1. Where correction of a written answer on the OMR is unavoidable, a single line through the incorrect word(s) is quite sufficient; there is no need to 'block out' mistakes and correcting fluid should not be used. Students with particularly large hand-writing may need practice in moderating their style to deal comfortably with the answer sheet. If blanks remain at the end of the paper, it is better to guess than to leave a question unanswered.

For **Paper 3** students should be advised to answer directly onto the answer sheet, to avoid copying errors, as accuracy is very important. The required answers to the five parts take the following forms:
Part 1 Shade in the lozenge of the correct option A, B, C or D in pencil.
Part 2 Write **one word only** (preferably in ink).

Part 3 Write between **two** and **five** words (preferably in ink).
Part 4 Tick (✔) correct lines; write **one word only** for incorrect lines (preferably in ink).
Part 5 Write one word only (preferably in ink).

For **Paper 4,** time is allowed at the end of the paper for transfer of answers, so students should write on the question paper and ignore the OMR until the last five minutes.

   The required answers to the five parts take the following forms:
Part 1 Shade in the lozenge of the correct option A, B or C in pencil.
Part 2 Write a word or short phrase (preferably in ink). Complete sentences are never required.
Part 3 Shade in the lozenge of the correct option A, B, C, D, E or F in pencil.
Part 4 Write the letter of the correct option (preferably in ink). These may vary from test to test.

Paper 2

Answers should be written in ink in the spaces provided on the question paper. The question number, but not the question, should be written at the beginning of the answer to Part 2. Organisation of content is assessed, so attention should be paid to punctuation, and paragraphing should be clear. No particular formats are expected, however. The report, for example, need not follow the conventions of formal business style. Although legibility is not assessed as such, work which is difficult to read will not improve students' chances of a good mark.

   Careful planning of answers will help students to avoid messy and disorganised work. Where amendments are necessary, they should be made as neatly as possible, indicating material which is to be ignored by crossing out with a single line *not* by using brackets.

Marking and grading

General procedures

All five papers of the FCE examination carry equal weighting. Each of the five papers is marked out of a different total, but the scores are weighted by computer so that each paper contributes 20 per cent to the total mark.

Each paper is marked in a slightly different way. Samples of OMR answer sheets for Papers 1, 3 and 4 appear at the back of the Student's Book.

The Reading paper is marked by an optical mark reader (OMR). The OMR sheets are scanned by the reader which is programmed with the correct keys.

The Writing paper is marked by EFL examiners who are trained and monitored through a co-ordination process.

The Use of English paper is marked by a combination of clerical marking and OMR. **Part 1** is marked by an OMR as for the Reading paper. The other parts have a tightly controlled mark-scheme which allows for clerical marking.

The Listening paper is marked by a combination of clerical marking and OMR. **Parts 1** and **3** are marked by an OMR. The other parts are clerically marked according to a tightly controlled mark-scheme.

The Speaking paper is assessed by two examiners.

The scores on the five components are added together by a computer after scaling. The final 'aggregate' mark determines the candidate's grade.

Results slip

Each candidate receives a results slip which tells them what grade they have achieved. This is in the range from A through to E. A, B and C are passing grades; D and E are failing grades. Candidates who fail are given an indication of the papers in which their performance was very weak, while candidates who pass are told which papers they did really well in.

Assessment and marking of Paper 2

Successful FCE candidates will typically meet the following requirements in the Writing paper:
● The demands of the task should be achieved within the word limits, and all the main points should be covered.

- Awareness of the appropriate register for the task should be demonstrated and maintained.
- The text should be suitably set out using appropriate paragraphing and the ideas should be clearly linked.
- The range of structure and vocabulary should be adequate to fulfil the requirements of the task.
- Any errors of structure or vocabulary should not impede communication.
- Handwriting should be legible.
- The text should have a satisfactory effect on the target reader.

The most able candidates will typically produce a wide range of structures and vocabulary, making few errors in spelling and punctuation. Their answers will include relevant and possibly some original details. The text would have a positive or very positive effect on the reader.

Candidates who are below FCE standard are likely to demonstrate many of the following weaknesses in the Writing paper: use of a very limited range of structure and vocabulary; failure to meet all the requirements of the task; omission of relevant points; inappropriate lifting from the questions; inclusion of irrelevant material; number of words either far below 120 or well above 180; poor lay-out or organisation; little or no use of linking devices; lack of awareness of appropriate register. Their writing does not clearly communicate the message to the target reader and may therefore have a negative effect.

Sample answers: Book 1

The following pieces of writing have been selected from students' answers produced during trialling. In order to help teachers in assessing the work of their own students, marks out of a possible total of 20 have been awarded based on the assessment criteria for the examination. Explanatory notes have been added to show how these marks have been arrived at. In this scoring system, successful candidates should normally expect to score 11 and above out of 20.

Sample answer A

Question answered: Book 1 Test 2 Part 2 Question 2

Mark: 18 out of 20

Comments: Good appreciation of the task set with well-conceived execution. Varied and generally well-expressed ideas with some successful attempts at more sophisticated language. Few errors, appropriate register and good control of complex structures.

Length: 154 words

Some weeks ago, I saw a film with the actor Tom Hanks. The film is called "Forest Gump" and I really enjoyed it. It's about the life of a person whose name is Forest Gump. Gump is not very intelligent and he has been teased by other people during his whole life. However, he has always had luck and in the end, he becomes very popular even though he didn't do anything for being famous.

From my point of view, the actor Tom Hanks plays his part excellently. You really must love the character he plays. Although Gump is a dull person who doesn't understand what occurs around him, he's always in the centre of events.

Personally I liked this film very much because it gives evidence of the society in general. You must read between the line. If you're not able to look in depth you will think the film is just silly.

Sample answer B

Question answered: Book 1 Test 3 Part 1 Question 1

Mark: 16 out of 20

Comments: Successful handling of the task with information well selected and integrated. Varied sentence structure and generally accurate grammar, presenting no major problems for the reader.

Length: 179 words

Dear Paul,

I'm writing to give you some news about the holiday I'm spending in Greece.

Since I arrived nine days ago, I've done all sorts of things, like sports, sightseeing tours, and going to a disco or a cinema in the evening. One exciting experience was sailing for the first time in my life. I know you enjoy doing that sport, so this is one reason I think it would be nice to come back together next year.

If the weather doesn't permit to go on the beach, I can have a swim in one of the pools belonging to the hotel; there are a lot of young people doing the same things and it's easy to get to know them. Also the family who run the hotel are very friendly and the food is quite good.

I can't write now about all the activities provided; I'll tell you about them when I get back next week, and I hope to persuade you to share this experience next time.

I look forward to seeing you soon,

Bye,

xxxx

Sample answer C

Question answered: Book 1 Test 3 Part 1 Question 1

Mark: 15 out of 20

Comments: Generally clear, but with a consistent level of minor error. Task competently handled but with little attempt at development.

Length: 176 words

Dear Sandra,

I'm now on holiday at the Bayview Hotel. Everything is wonderful and I've a really good time. The hotel is all I need; a restaurant with delicious food, bar and two pools.

As soon as I arrived to the Bayview I decided to come back next year and I would like you to come with me. We could have so much fun together here. It's a cinema, discos and a lot of shops near the hotel and we can always go for a walk in the mountains or try sailing. Tomorrow I'm going to sail, it's the first time for me and I'm looking foreward to it.

Apart from that, the hotel organize trips every day to interesting places. On Tuesday I'm going by coach to the old town and a museum.

Finally the best thing is that the hotel is very cheap so why don't you come with me? Think about it and tell me your decision next month.

I'm looking foreward to hearing from you!

        Love,

           XXXX

Sample answer D

Question answered: Book 1 Test 3 Part 2 Question 4

Mark: 13 out of 20

Comments: Reasonable treatment of task. Regular errors, some of which might cause problems for non-specialist readers, but most ideas clearly communicated. Simple, repetitive sentence structure.

Length: 171 words

One evening I went with my husband to the local restaurant near where we lives. It's an Italian restaurant, there you can eat lots of pizza and pasta. We can't complain about the food, because we had a lovely dinner. There were plenty of dishes you could choose between. and it wasn't so expensive either. the restaurant it selves is very nice and the atmosphere is very pleased. There are always lot's of customers and the waiters are all the time busy. "That was the problem". It took an hour before we could order and we had to wait a long time before we got the bill. Meanwhile the waiters looked like they were going to get a heart attack. I and my husband felt very sorry for them. So we didn't want to make a complaint.

In conclusion we recommend it for you who have time to wait, because the dinner is splended.

The restaurant is named Roma and is situated on Hannover Street.

We hope you enjoy your food.

Marking and grading

Sample answer E

Question answered:	Book 1 Test 4 Part 1 Question 1
Mark:	11 out of 20
Comments:	Overlong, largely due to preoccupation with detailed directions. Register deteriorates steadily from good tone in first paragraph to very casual last sentence. Some basic errors, but does achieve task.
Length:	226 words

Dear Mr John Stevens,

I'm writing to confirm my invite to the Swansea College to talk about "The Industrial Revolution in South Wales" – I'm sorry to tell you that it's impossible for me to meet your train because it arrives at 16.45 and I'm busy until 17.00. Apologising for not being able to take you at the station, I would like to suggest you the different ways to arrive at the School, so that you can choose the best.

If you prefer going on foot, this is possible because the School is not so far from the station: you could go down High Street and take the first turning on the right and then go straight on Alexandra Road – you'll pass the library on the left At the first corner on the right you'll find the Fire Station, turn there and go straight ahead until you get to the School on the right – Another possibilty is taking a bus: the bus stop is in front of the Station and you can get off the bus at the Mount Pleasant Hospital; then you can go back on the same street on foot until you can see the School on your left.

If you are tired or in late, you could take a taxi on High Street only a few metres far from the station.

Yours, faithfully
XXXX

Sample answer F

Question answered:	Book 1 Test 4 Part 2 Question 2
Mark:	7 out of 20
Comments:	Nature of task entirely misunderstood: by presenting a whole meal, the candidate effectively minimises the opportunity for *instructional* language, which is the intended task focus. Consistent level of basic error. Overuse of non-English terms with little attempt to explain or contextualise.
Length:	205 words

Dear Patty

Thank you for your last letter. I'm very interested in your idea about having a traditional lunch of my country for celebrate your friend's birthday. I'm writing for giving you some advice.

I'm sure you are a small group of people, so you will have a good result. the meal that I have chosen is very simple, but remember to take care carefully at the preparation of the receipeits.

I suggest you to start with several "crostini" with jam like appetizers, then go on with "spaghetti al pomodoro". You ought to cook the tomatoes with garlic in oil just only few minutes and add some bazil at the end. As regards the main course you should prepare "melanzane alla parmigiana" with roasted pork steak. the slices of vegetables have been cooked in a pan put in the oven with the slices of "mozzarella" and grated "parmigiano" for us! As for cakes is concerned you ought to prepare an apple cake.

I hope you're satisfied with my instructions. I'm sure that if you follow me my advice your guest will keen on the meal.

As soon as possible, give me the news about you and obviously how the lunch's gone

With my best wishes from
XXXXX

Sample answer G

Question answered:	Book 1 Test 3 Part 2 Question 4
Mark:	4 out of 20
Comments:	Task entirely misunderstood, resulting in first person narrative, where a more general report is called for. Consistently poor control of grammar and sentence structure. Communication breaks down completely towards end.
Length:	124 words

A local newspaper invited some readers for lunch in a local restaurant. I was one of them and I decided to go.

We arrived at the restaurant it was outside from the city and it was quite small. I was simply but the atmosphere was very friendly. I had a fine place the tables were round and it had vase with flowers on them. The staff welcome us and serviced. The food was excellent Except an event which happened. One of the waiter when he served fall down a glass of wine on me, when the boss of the restaurant saw that came near he told to him in front of us You're fired.

It was very rude to fire an employee like this.

Sample answers: Book 2

The following pieces of writing have been selected from students' answers produced during trialling. In order to help teachers in assessing the work of their own students, marks out of a possible total of 20 have been awarded based on the assessment criteria for the examination. Explanatory notes have been added to show how these marks have been arrived at. In this scoring system, successful candidates should normally expect to score 11 and above out of 20.

Sample answer A

Question answered: Book 2 Test 4 Part 1 Question 1

Mark: 19 out of 20

Comments: Well-tailored answer dealing with all significant areas of the task. Tenses incorrect when dealing with hypothetical ideas, but otherwise very few errors. Generally comfortable expression and suitable register throughout.

Length: 169 words

Dear Miss Tabacek,

I am very sorry to tell you that your friend will not be able to come to the course which begins next week. I received your message this morning and I am afraid nothing can be done now. There are no more coaches for the sightseeing tours planned or theatre tickets available and she will miss a very important part of the course without them.

But the main problem is that your friend doesn't have the English level required for the course. As there are going to be daily lectures in English, in which specific language will be used, she won't be able to understand them. In addition, you probably told her this course cost a very reasonable price, but it is much more expensive now without the discount we got on accommodation when we booked them last year.

I don't think your friend should be with us this year but I sincerely hope she will in the future.

Looking forward to see you here next week

Yours sincerely,

Sample answer B

Question answered:	Book 2 Test 2 Part 2 Question 2
Mark:	16 out of 20
Comments:	Slightly overlong, but execution of task well-structured and under complete control. Clear expression throughout, supported by some more sophisticated language and structure. Few errors, which do not impede communication.
Length:	190 words

Once I heard from my friend about the book entitled „The hunt for Red October", I was very curious what the book was about so I decided to read it.

Generally I don't like sensational books but the further I was reading the more it seemed interesting. The book is about an escape of the most modern Russian submarine with nuclear missiles on deck to United States.

There are several important problems in this book. Firstly, will the Russian navy regain or sink their submarine or will the Americans conquer it? Secondly, the captain Marco Romius is the best commander in the Russian navy. There is a competition between the teacher and the apprentice. Victor Tupelev, the most clever of Romius' apprentices, now the commander of submarine „Alfa" has to prevent his ex-teacher from escaping to the USA. Thirdly, the Americans have to foresee the next move of Romius and help him to get to their country. Lastly the action is so fast it seems almost impossible.

I think that even persons who don't like such stories should have this book in their home-libraries, because it is really worth reading.

Sample answer C

Question answered: Book 2 Test 3 Part 2 Question 3

Mark: 15 out of 20

Comments: Over length, but otherwise competent approach to task. Narrative framework well-handled. Evidence of careless slips; the candidate might well have done better by writing to the prescribed length and using the time saved to check for errors.

Length: 207 words

It is often suggested that most of the people don't care anymore about other persons problems and that our society is getting worse and worse. But fortunately there are always exceptions to every rule.

I leave the University at 5p.m. on Fridays. That Friday I was particularly tired and I decided to go back home by taxi instead of by bus. The taxi driver was a very talkative man and you know how irritating it is someone talking to you in a loud voice if you have a headache.

When I was inside my house I realized that I had left my bag inside the car. I felt very depressed and I assumed that I wouldn't have my things back. But surprisingly on Saturday morning a man rang the bell. It was the taxi driver with my bag. I thanked him and asked if I could do anything for him, but he said he was in a hurry. When I opened the bag everything was in its place and there wasn't even a single peny missed.

I wanted to share my story with the other readers to let them know that there are still people who help each other without looking for a benefit of any kind.

Sample answer D

Question answered:	Book 2 Test 3 Part 2 Question 2
Mark:	14 out of 20
Comments:	Simple, but quite effective treatment of task, covering several points, but with little attempt at development. Communicates clearly and accurately, but fairly basic vocabulary throughout.
Length:	162 words

If there is somebody I will never forget, he is my grandfather. Although he died when I was only nine years old, he has had a big influence on me.

He was the most quiet person I have ever known. I think he was a little shy too. But when you got to know him really, you realized what a wonderful person he was. He always knew the right thing to say when I felt unhappy and he was the only one who could make me laugh when I was angry. We used to spend a lot of time talking and playing cards together. He was a very old man but he was as happy and as inocent as the youngest boy. He was the one who played with me the most and the only person I felt I could tell all my secrets.

My grandfather has been very important to me and I wish I could be like him some day.

Sample answer E

Question answered:	Book 2 Test 3 Part 1 Question 1
Mark:	12 out of 20
Comments:	Basic elements of task achieved. Formal register attempted, but without any great certainty. Rambling sentence structure threatens to impede communication at key points.
Length:	134 words

Dear Mr Brian McConnell,

I am writing to complain about the last information I received of the changes in the Ocean Hotel last week.

First, I would like to express my displeasure about the bad management of the company for not inform before about the possibilities of the changes in the holiday I have booked.

Furthermore, I didn't expect to receive this kind of information just two weeks before my family and I are due to travel. In this holiday were included all the sports and entertainment which were the main reason of buying the "Carefree Holiday". So, I recommend that you should give me my money back or show me other holiday where my family and I can do swimming sports for the same price.

Please be sure that this kind of accident won't happen again.

Yours sincerely,

Sample answer F

Question answered:	Book 2 Test 3 Part 1 Question 1
Mark:	10 out of 20
Comments:	Task achieved, though some points under-developed. Contains a number of fixed phrases, accurately and appropriately used, but these cannot mask the fragility of the free composition, where errors are basic and frequent.
Length:	136 words

Dear Mr McConnell,

I am writing to inform you of my extreme displeasure upon receiving your letter regarding the changes to the holiday I have booked.

Your letter makes an absolute mockery of the advertisement which convince me to book a holiday with you, and I would like to draw to you attention the following points:

1) Instead of being accommodated in brand news luxury accomodation I will be placed in a half finished complex, with building work as doubt being disruptive and noisy.

2) Instead of having big name bands and a swimming pool only limited entertainments will be provided and then only in the second week.

3) The world famous chef quoted in your advertisement has now become a nearby restaurant.

I therefore wish cancel my holiday and demand a full refind of my deposite.

Yours Sincerely,

Sample answer G

Question answered:	Book 2 Test 1 Part 2 Question 3
Mark:	9 out of 20
Comments:	Far too long; task not under control: dwells on general background at the expense of the actual answer to the question. The most relevant material appears *after* the 180 words specified in the question, demonstrating the importance of forward planning. Regular errors and uncertain sentence structure make it hard to follow the development at times.
Length:	253 words

I work all day in a rather dirty and quite dark office. I have been working there for three months more or less and I want to change this job but nowadays is very difficult to find a better one. They don't pay me as I would like to but I live with my parents so I can keep all the money. I have three workmates which are working there for a long time. At first I thought they would be very good friends but then I realised I was wrong. They treat me like a stranger but they never talk to me or say 'good morning' when I arrive. I've been thinking of talk to them but it isn't worth doing it. I was looking forward to find another job because I wouldn't support this climate anymore. But last Monday something strange happened. When I arrived to the office everyone said to me 'Hello' in a very polite way. I didn't understand what was happening. When I sat on my desk I found a cup of coffee and a chocolate. I couldn't believe my eyes. When I asked what happened nobody told me anything. When I was leaving one of them told me that they want to talk to the boss but they didn't dare. They wanted me to talk to him. They wanted to change the office because it was very old and they couldn't work there anymore. All at once I began to understand why I was being treated so well.

Sample answer H

Question answered:	Book 2 Test 2 Part 2 Question 4
Mark:	8 out of 20
Comments:	Overlong. Task misunderstood, as confirmed by final sentence. Too much emphasis on the 'stay', not much evidence of 'excitement'. Generally quite easy to follow, despite some persistent errors.
Length:	211 words

It all happened a year ago when I was traveling to Edinburgh. I have been very excited from the very begining as it was my first travel abroad on my own.

We started off from Warsaw at 8am on an extremely hot day and got to Calais the next morning with no problem. We finally got to London at about lunch-time. I bought myself a ticket to Edinburgh. The coach was to leave Victoria station at 23.45. I have left my things in the left-luggage office and decided to wonder around London. I have spent the rest of the day talking to some extremely nice people and visiting some fascinating places. The next day, finally in Edinburgh, I met my wonderful host family – Scotish father, Venezuelian mother and three little „devils"– their children.

I have spent a fantastic month in the Scotland's capital, heaving made a lot of friends (we still do corespondate), attending my course of English and the Edinburgh Festival as well. As I stayed just next door to the castle, I did not need a pass to see some events on the castle's courtyard. I have also visited Scotish Highlands a few times.

It was certainly my most exciting holiday, which I shall never forget.

Sample answer I

Question answered: Book 2 Test 1 Part 1 Question 1

Mark: 6 out of 20

Comments: Task understood, but errors obscure meaning at key points. Staccato sentences, disjointed structure and little attempt to develop ideas.

Length: 181 words

Dear Stephen,

I'm writing to tell you how foolish your brother idea is going to Merle Park with his children.

Firstly I would like to remembered you the bad time I spent in that place. It was awful! You had to be there at 6.00AM because that was the time the pools were open and also the time that the training began, and if you weren't there you were considered absent.

Also I remembered one time I was coming from a full training day and they invited me an excursion of local beauty spots. It was really boring and I decided to go immediatly.

I think your brother must be out of brains if he decides to go to that place. Even the games for children were boring, can you imagine that? They told us they had a wave machine. If it really exists I didn't see it.

So if you want an opinion for someone who has already been there I will sume it up in two words NO WAY. Send my regards to your family and your crazy brother.

Yours, sincerely

Sample answer J

Question answered:	Book 2 Test 3 Part 1 Question 1
Mark:	3 out of 20
Comments:	Language level insufficient to accomplish task in any meaningful sense for non-specialist reader. Little attempt to use given information. Punctuation errors compound the effects of ambiguity and grammatical weakness.
Length:	122 words

Dear Mr B McConnell

I regret to inform you. It is quite diffulent between your letter and your advertisement. I am afraid, I do not want to have a holiday. Could you tell me why you changed our plan and why you do not tell us before paying? I suppose you have not got a right of changing it for us. And also your advertisement has been written any limits. I hope I would like to be my money back, because I am not interested about my holiday anymore. I would like to have a holiday next time, when your advertisement is perfect.

I would like to hearing from you as sonn as possible and to being arranged my wish, please.

Yours sincerely

Assessment and marking of Paper 5

Candidates are assessed according to the following criteria:
- Linguistic resource (including control of appropriate structures and the use of varied and appropriate vocabulary)
- Pronunciation of sentences, words and individual sounds (for example, rhythm and intonation patterns, stressed and unstressed sounds)
- Fluency (speed and rhythm, choice of structures, general naturalness and clarity)
- Interactive communication (for example, turn-taking, holding the floor, negotiating meaning, initiating and responding)
- Task achievement (that is, treatment of the task in terms of coherence, organisation of main points and appropriateness of language).

Successful FCE candidates will typically meet the following requirements in the Speaking paper:
- sufficient range and control of structures to deal adequately with the task
- adequate range and control of vocabulary to talk about subjects of general interest and to achieve the task
- pronunciation foreign but enough control over pronunciation of individual sounds, stress-timing, rhythm, and placing of stress and intonation in words and sentences to achieve broad understanding
- discussion of the task without so much hesitation that communication is impeded
- sufficient sensitivity to turn-taking, ability to initiate discussion and respond to questions, negotiate and elaborate meaning where required.

The most able candidates will typically have control over a wide range of structures with few gaps in vocabulary for everyday situations; pronunciation may be foreign-sounding but very easily understood; natural hesitation; full and natural contribution to the interaction with occasional minor difficulties in turn-taking or negotiation; effective, comprehensive and independent treatment of the task.

Candidates who are below FCE standard are likely to demonstrate many of the following features: inaccurate use of structures; insufficient range and inaccurate use of vocabulary; pronunciation which makes them difficult to understand; unacceptable hesitation which strains the listener; difficulty in contributing to and maintaining a discussion; inadequate or irrelevant attempts at the task requiring too much redirection or assistance.

Book 1 Test 1 Key

Paper 1 Reading

Part 1

1 C   2 F   3 H   4 A   5 G   6 E   7 B

Part 2

8 B   9 D   10 A   11 B   12 D   13 B   14 A   15 C

Part 3

16 B   17 D   18 G   19 E   20 A   21 C

Part 4

22 and 23 A/C   24 B   25 C   26 F   27 and 28 D/H   29 D
30 G   31 C   32 A   33 and 34 E/G   35 H
(Where there are two possible answers, these are interchangeable.)

Paper 3 Use of English

Award one mark for each correct answer, except in Part 3, where two marks are available, divided up as shown, for each answer.

Correct spelling is essential throughout. Ignore omission or abuse of capital letters. No half marks.

Part 1

1 B   2 A   3 C   4 D   5 A   6 D   7 D   8 B
9 C   10 A   11 D   12 C   13 B   14 A   15 A

Part 2

16 where   17 how   18 anyone/anybody   19 tried/attempted/threatened
20 after   21 no   22 a/per/each/every   23 The   24 whose
25 yet/but/(al)though   26 of   27 as   28 If/Provided/Providing
29 to   30 will/can

Part 3

31 accused Frank of (1) breaking/having broken (1)
32 must have/get (1) my car (1)
33 wishes she (1) had bought (1)
34 if you (1) hadn't/had not helped (1) OR but for/without you/your (1) helping (1)
35 in case (1) I ran (1)
36 have fallen (1) through (1)

37 wasn't/was not (1) fresh enough (1)
38 may have (1) gone (1)
39 is/'s impossible (1) for me to (1)
40 was (1) being watched (1)

Part 4

41 much   **42** until   **43** ✓   **44** it   **45** myself   **46** one
47 ✓   **48** ✓   **49** out   **50** to   **51** ✓   **52** with   **53** so
54 all   **55** for

Part 5

56 life   **57** noticing   **58** originally   **59** convenience   **60** sale
61 widened   **62** shorter   **63** underground   **64** likelihood
65 freedom

Paper 4 Listening

Part 1

1 B   **2** C   **3** B   **4** A   **5** B   **6** A   **7** B   **8** A

Part 2

9 useful for future/helpful for career/wants to be a nurse *etc.*
10 farmhouse   **11** road   **12** lifts   **13** (taking round) evening drinks
14 money/costs *etc.*   **15** grateful (for extras)   **16** her son-in-law
17 (an) equal/(just) the same (as them)   **18** organise (a) concert

Part 3

19 B   **20** A   **21** C   **22** F   **23** E

Part 4

24 T   **25** T   **26** T   **27** F   **28** T   **29** F   **30** F

Transcript *First Certificate Practice Test One. Paper Four. Listening. Hello, I'm going to give you the instructions for this test. I'll introduce each part of the test and give you time to look at the questions. At the start of each piece, you'll hear this sound:*

tone

You'll hear each piece twice.

Remember, while you're listening, write your answers on the question paper. You'll have time at the end of the test to copy your answers onto the separate answer sheet.
The tape will now be stopped. Please ask any questions now, because you must not speak during the test.

[pause]

PART 1 *Now, open your question paper and look at Part One.*
You'll hear people talking in eight different situations. For questions 1 to 8,
choose the best answer, A, B or C.

Question 1 One
You are visiting a museum when you hear this man addressing a group of
people. Who is he?
A a security guard
B a tourist guide
C a museum guide

[pause]

tone

Tourist guide: O.K. everyone, uh, before we go into the next room I'd like to warn you not to try and touch any of the wall-hangings or furniture. As you will see they're very beautiful, with very delicate finishes. The museum is very strict about this and they will ask you to leave if they think you're not taking the rule seriously. I actually had someone told to leave when I brought a group here last year because he accidentally brushed against something. Um?

[pause]

tone

[The recording is repeated.]

[pause]

Question 2 Two
You're in a restaurant when you overhear one of the waiters talking. Who is
he talking about?
A a colleague
B the manager
C a customer

[pause]

tone

Waiter: Well, I said, I don't stand for that sort of thing from anyone. I don't care whether they've been coming here since before I was born, they've no right to speak to anyone like that. I'm doing my job and it's my job to serve her a meal, not run up and down the road with messages. She's going to complain about me she said. Well, I'm going to complain about her!

[pause]

tone

[The recording is repeated.]

[pause]

Question 3   *Three*
You're waiting in a hospital corridor when you hear this woman talking.
What does she say about her doctor?
A He's made a mistake.
B He's been unhelpful.
C He's been untruthful.

[pause]

tone

Woman: To be honest I thought at first he'd got my notes mixed up with someone else. We didn't seem to be talking about the same illness. He kept going on about how it's not uncommon for these side-effects to occur. And I thought, that's all very well for you to say, but I'm the only case I know, and I asked what he was going to do now. Well, he just sort of smiled, and said something about 'weighing discomfort against disease', really pompous! And that was it as far as he was concerned.

[pause]

tone

[The recording is repeated.]

[pause]

Question 4   *Four*
You are out shopping when you hear a shop assistant talking to a customer.
What is she refusing to do?
A give him some money
B change a faulty item
C repair something

[pause]

tone

Shop assistant: Unfortunately, it's just not possible for me to do that. I don't have the authority, you see.
Man: But, but, it's faulty. I know my rights.
Shop assistant: But I can't tell if there's really anything wrong with it, just looking at it, so the best I can do is give you a credit note as if you'd changed your mind about wanting it. Then you can choose goods to the same value, well, either now or at a later date. Because we don't give cash refunds unless there's something actually wrong with the item. Otherwise, I can have it sent back for checking, but I still can't pay anything out till we've had confirmation of a fault.

[pause]

tone

[The recording is repeated.]

[pause]

Question 5   *Five*
Listen to this woman introducing the next speaker at a conference. Why has
she been asked to introduce him?
A He is an old friend.
B He is a former student of hers.
C He is a colleague.

[pause]

tone

Conference chair: Now, it gives me the greatest pleasure to introduce our keynote speaker. I take no small pride in having had even a minor role in the development of one of the most forward-thinking workers in his field. We shared many fascinating discussions as he raced through my course, too many years ago now. I can hardly claim to have taught, merely to have helped along the way, although he has been kind enough to say he learnt from me! Anyway, I'm very honoured to present to you ….

[pause]

tone

[The recording is repeated.]

[pause]

Question 6   *Six*
You are staying in a farmhouse when you hear your host on the telephone.
Who is he talking to?
A a supplier
B a customer
C an employee

[pause]

tone

Farmer: No, no, I'm sorry, I simply can't accept that. I'm running a business here, too, and I can't just turn round and tell my customers that, well, sorry, no vegetables this week, I haven't had time to pick them! I've got fields here waiting to be planted out. You've been telling me for a week you'd have the fertiliser in stock tomorrow. I need it on that field today. If you can't get it here I'll have to find someone else who can.

[pause]

tone

[The recording is repeated.]

[pause]

Question 7   *Seven*
You hear this critic talking on the radio. What is she recommending?
A a film
B a book
C an exhibition

[pause]

tone

Critic: I was really pleased to be asked to review this, because I was enormously curious to see whether Delaney could handle the change of medium, whether he could colour in the bits between the dialogue, so to speak. In fact I think he's done very well, and there's no sign of that horrid 'book of the film' feel that you sometimes get from people who are crossing over from script-writing to the novel. The characters are very finely drawn and right from the first chapter the plot is cleverly worked. I have some little doubts about ...

[pause]

tone

[The recording is repeated.]

[pause]

Question 8   *Eight*
You are walking up the street when you hear this man talking to a woman at her front door. What does he want to do?
A interview her
B help her
C advise her

[pause]

tone

Reporter: I won't keep you more than a few minutes, and I'm sure if you think about it, you'll realise that talking to someone like me will be a lot better than leaving people to make everything up. Because I can assure you, they will make it up, if you don't get your story out first, so why not just give me your side of things now?

[pause]

tone

[The recording is repeated.]

[pause]

That's the end of Part One.
Now turn to Part Two.

PART 2   *You will hear a student called Bill talking about his holiday job. For questions 9 to 18, complete the notes which summarise what he says. You will need to write a word or a short phrase. You now have forty-five seconds in which to look at Part Two.*

[pause]

tone

Bill: Yeah, over last summer I did this job in an old people's home. I'd been looking for work and I said I wanted something which might be useful, because I want to train as a nurse when I finish school, so they said what about a care assistant, and I said, sure. So, anyway, I went along and it's in this old house, it was a farmhouse, but the farm's all gone, now the town's got bigger, and it's just got a bit of a garden round it. It's got a lawn and flowerbeds at the back, but the front is quite near the road. I was surprised but the old people like it they say, because they can watch what's going on a bit. You know, some places, they're very pretty, but so quiet and they feel cut off. It's quite a nice building, with lots of the old woodwork and so on, just they've put in a couple of lifts for obvious reasons, because they've got some quite frail people among the residents.

I really liked the work, which was a relief, and I got on pretty well with most of the residents. Some of them were a good laugh. They like talking about when they were younger. The best part of my work was when I'd take round their evening drinks, I wouldn't be having to rush off, and I could take time to listen. I suppose they'd told all their stories before but I hadn't heard them, so I was a good audience.

I didn't see much of Mrs Stone, that's the owner, but she seemed all right. She's got two or three of these places, and I think she's always concerned about whether she's going to lose money. But I don't think she's mean. She just can't afford not to be businesslike about it, or they'd go bust. The residents mostly seemed to like her, anyway. They were nice, most of them, one or two of the old girls could be a bit snappy, but I think that was their arthritis, and the old boys were all ever so grateful if you had time to do them any little extras. The only really tricky one was this old girl who thought I was her son-in-law, because of my hair being the same colour, and she didn't get on with her son-in-law, so she didn't get on with me. But I survived, anyway. The rest of the staff did what they could. It was really good, being treated just the same, like an equal, by very experienced people. It made me value my own work and try to do it as well as them. It was a really useful experience, and I learnt a lot. I'm going back there next month, because I'm organising a concert for them. They're looking forward to it. And what I wanted to ask, was whether anyone …

[pause]

tone

Now you'll hear Part Two again.

[The recording is repeated.]

[pause]

That's the end of Part Two.
Now turn to Part Three.

PART 3   *You will hear five different women talking about parties.*
For questions 19 to 23, choose from the list A to F what they describe. Use
the letters only once. There is one extra letter which you do not need to use.
You now have 30 seconds in which to look at Part Three.

[pause]

tone

First woman: I must admit that I was extremely reluctant. You know I don't go out much these days, I don't see many people and I tend to think that anything with more than a handful of people will be noisy and exhausting. But it was really pleasant. There was masses of room, lovely things to eat and drink, and when I discovered it was gone midnight I was amazed. The time had flown and I hadn't noticed.

[pause]

Second woman: Well, they said, Come on, you know how people do, so I went, I didn't want them to think I was being an old misery. After all, I don't often see them since we left college. But, I swear, that's the last time I let them drag me anywhere. I don't think they thought it was much fun either, though they wouldn't admit it of course, but I haven't been so bored for years. I should've stayed at home watching the rubbish on telly!

[pause]

Third woman: So anyway, they all decided they'd come too. And I said, 'But were you invited?' And they said, well, I don't know, they sort of implied they were. So I turned up with them and the girl who was giving the party, you don't know her, she's very nice, anyway she came to the door, and said 'Hello' to me and sort of looked at the others and then looked at me and I realised she thought I was taking advantage, and I went all hot and cold. Anyway we went in and I could see her looking at me from time to time, and I thought, well she won't ask me again, and I was longing to explain but I never had a chance. It was horrible. I'll never forgive them.

[pause]

Fourth woman: We all arrived and my friends went off to find drinks and things and I was just standing there feeling shy as usual and thinking, 'Why did I come?' And I saw this girl watching me, and I thought she'd noticed something wrong, so I was sort of checking myself in a mirror, trying not to look as if I was, then she came up and asked if I was Suzanne, and I said I was, and then she started on about my work. She knew all about it and said a lot of flattering things, in a very nice way. I enjoyed meeting her, she really made the evening for me. I wish I'd remembered to find out where she lived.

[pause]

Fifth woman: It was nearly a disaster. I mean, I wouldn't have missed the opportunity to meet him, but I'd had no idea it'd be swarming with children. And we were outdoors most of the time, so of course I was freezing, because I'd only got a shawl over my dress, trying to look smart. I needn't have bothered of course. Anyway, I, I did enjoy talking to him, although it wasn't for long enough really, and the food was wonderful. But, um, I think I'll swallow my pride and phone and check another time!

[pause]

tone

Now you'll hear Part Three again.

[The recording is repeated.]

[pause]

That's the end of Part Three.
Now turn to Part Four.

PART 4   *You will hear a conversation between two teenagers, Nick and Sandra.*
Decide whether statements 24 to 30 are true or false and mark your answers
T for True or F for False. You now have forty-five seconds in which to look at
Part Four.

[pause]

tone

Nick:	Hi, Sandra, where've you been?
Sandra:	Oh, am I late? Sorry. I had to do some tidying up before I came out.
Nick:	Yeah, I know. I hate getting home and finding I've still got to wash up from breakfast.
Sandra:	It's not me that minds. It's my mother. She treats me like I was twelve or something. You've no idea how lucky you are to have your own place.
Nick:	Well, you'd have to do it eventually, wouldn't you?
Sandra:	I don't see why. It's my room, she doesn't have to come poking in there and telling me what to do.
Nick:	Well, I guess if you don't mind the mess and it's just your room, then I suppose she should let you. Personally, I like to be able to find things in a hurry.
Sandra:	I can find things when I want to. What really gets me is she makes me do all sorts of stupid chores every Saturday round the house.
Nick:	Well, she can't do them all.
Sandra:	She isn't going anywhere. She's got all weekend to do them.
Nick:	Oh, come on. Why should she do housework all weekend while you enjoy yourself?
Sandra:	She hasn't got exams next month. I haven't got time.
Nick:	I think you're being a bit unreasonable. You have time to come and meet me.
Sandra:	That's different.
Nick:	No, it isn't.
Sandra:	Whose side are you on, here?
Nick:	Look, perhaps I just have a better idea how much your Mum has to get through. When you're responsible for a place it makes a lot of difference.
Sandra:	Oh, don't be such a pain. Are you going to keep lecturing me all evening or are we going to see this band?
Nick:	Sure. Have you brought the tickets?
Sandra:	What tickets?
Nick:	I got them on Thursday and gave them to you to look after. Don't you remember? You put them in your jeans pocket.
Sandra:	You're teasing me. Oh no! Mum washed these jeans yesterday. I bet she never checked the pockets. Oh, I'll kill her!
Nick:	Well, have a look. Anyway, I don't see why she should check your pockets.

Sandra: Okay, okay. Don't start that again. Oh no, wait a minute, this might be them. Do you think they're all right? They're a bit crumpled.

Nick: Honestly! Next time I'd better look after them myself. I'm sure they'll be OK. Now, get a move on, or we won't get in after all this.

[pause]

tone

Now you'll hear Part Four again.

[The recording is repeated.]

[pause]

That is the end of Part Four.
There'll now be a pause of five minutes for you to copy your answers onto the separate answer sheet.
I'll remind you when there's one minute left, so that you're sure to finish in time.

[pause]

You have one more minute left.

[pause]

That's the end of the test. Please stop now. Your supervisor will now collect all the question papers and answer sheets.
Goodbye.

Book 1 Test 2 Key

Paper 1 Reading

Part 1
1 C   2 H   3 D   4 A   5 G   6 F   7 B

Part 2
8 C   9 C   10 B   11 A   12 C   13 D   14 B   15 A

Part 3
16 G   17 A   18 C   19 E   20 D   21 B

Part 4
22 B   23 D   24 E   25 H   26 and 27 G/H   28 A
29 D   30 C   31 B   32 E   33 and 34 A/E   35 C
(Where there are two possible answers, these are interchangeable.)

Paper 3 Use of English

Award one mark for each correct answer, except in Part 3, where two marks are available, divided up as shown, for each answer.

Correct spelling is essential throughout. Ignore omission or abuse of capital letters. No half marks.

Part 1
1 C   2 D   3 A   4 B   5 D   6 B   7 A   8 A
9 C   10 D   11 A   12 B   13 A   14 C   15 D

Part 2
16 as   17 how/what   18 it   19 into/to/through   20 or/and
21 since   22 by   23 the/those   24 of   25 been   26 In
27 are   28 this   29 which   30 fact

Part 3
31 whose coat (1) this (1) OR whose (1) this coat (1)
32 prevented her (1) (from) taking (1)
33 must not be (1) ridden (1) OR must be (1) pushed/carried/wheeled (1)
34 was amazed (1) to find (1)
35 don't need to/needn't/need not (1) book (1)
36 too high (1) for (any of) (1)
37 would/'d rather (1) you started (1)
38 they remembered (1) what (they had) (1)

64

39 hardly ever (1) loses her (1)
40 have/'ve run (1) out of (1)

Part 4

41 for   **42** the   **43** of   **44** ✓   **45** ✓   **46** more   **47** will
48 much   **49** ✓   **50** ever   **51** only   **52** ✓   **53** a   **54** at
55 it

Part 5

56 settlement   **57** southern   **58** earliest   **59** uninhabited
60 surrounded   **61** building   **62** religious   **63** successfully
64 development   **65** central

Paper 4 Listening

Part 1

1 B   **2** A   **3** C   **4** A   **5** C   **6** C   **7** A   **8** B

Part 2

9 (in the) suburbs   **10** librarian   **11** (about) once a week
12 should (stay) open later   **13** too high/not cheap   **14** need modernising
15 (more) showers   **16** athletics   **17** local business(es)
18 pensioners

Part 3

19 C   **20** D   **21** E   **22** B   **23** A

Part 4

24 T   **25** F   **26** F   **27** T   **28** T   **29** F   **30** F

Transcript   *First Certificate Practice Test Two. Paper Four. Listening. Hello, I'm going to give you the instructions for this test. I'll introduce each part of the test and give you time to look at the questions. At the start of each piece, you'll hear this sound:*

tone

You'll hear each piece twice.
Remember, while you're listening, write your answers on the question paper. You'll have time at the end of the test to copy your answers onto the separate answer sheet.
The tape will now be stopped. Please ask any questions now, because you must not speak during the test.

[pause]

PART 1　*Now, open your question paper and look at Part One.*
You'll hear people talking in eight different situations. For questions 1 to 8,
choose the best answer, A, B or C.

Question 1　One
You are walking round a market when you hear this woman talking to a
customer. What is she doing?
A asking the customer's opinion
B offering a cheap sample
C explaining a price rise

[pause]

tone

Market trader:　Look, I tell you what. You just take a couple home tonight, I'll knock off fifty pence,
how's that? And try them – you'll love 'em, I promise you – and then tomorrow you can
come and tell me if I'm not right. What d'you say to that, then? I can't say fairer than
that, now can I?

[pause]

tone

[The recording is repeated.]

[pause]

Question 2　Two
You're in the doctor's waiting room when you overhear the nurse on the
phone. Why didn't she send off the notes?
A She didn't know they were wanted.
B It isn't part of her job to do it.
C She didn't know which notes to send.

[pause]

tone

Nurse:　No, I haven't received anything. ... Well, I do, normally, but even if our receptionist had,
she'd have told me straight away. ... Of course I'll go and look the notes out now and
send them off straight away. Now, what was the patient's name again?

[pause]

tone

[The recording is repeated.]

[pause]

Question 3　Three
You're in a gallery when you hear these women talking. What are they
looking at?
A a bowl
B a lamp
C a vase

[pause]

tone

First woman:	It's very lovely, isn't it?
Second woman:	Well, I suppose so, but it's not really practical, is it? I mean, it's so tall and thin you'd be afraid of knocking it over. Or would you actually put flowers in it?
First woman:	Oh, really! You'd put it somewhere where the light could shine through, just to look at it. You wouldn't want to use it. Not at that price!

[pause]

tone

[The recording is repeated.]

[pause]

Question 4

Four
You are visiting a large company and you hear two people talking. What are they discussing?
A a personal computer
B a typewriter
C a CD player

[pause]

tone

Woman:	Look, we can put it here on the table.
Man:	Yes, that'll leave the desk clear for papers and things. But, er, will the light be OK? You don't want it reflecting on the screen.
Woman:	No, that's all right. I can turn it at an angle. Shall I go and get the disks and things?
Man:	No, don't bother, I'll bring them up later.

[pause]

tone

[The recording is repeated.]

[pause]

Question 5

Five
Listen to this clerk at a station booking office. Which is the cheapest ticket?
A a period return
B an ordinary return
C a Rover

[pause]

tone

|Railway clerk:|Well, you can either get a period return, if you're going to be away more than three nights, or you can get an ordinary return that leaves you free to come back any time, but of course it costs more, although it's cheaper than two singles, of course. Or you can get a Rover ticket, which allows unlimited travel within the region for up to seven|

days. That's cheaper than the period return, and you can go further, but of course not at rush hours.

[pause]

tone

[The recording is repeated.]

[pause]

Question 6   *Six*
These friends are talking about a film. Who will go to see it?
A   both of them
B   neither of them
C   the girl

[pause]

tone

Girl: I really think you ought to give it a chance. You aren't usually so narrow-minded.
Boy: I'm not. But Barry said his Dad really enjoyed it. We've got no tastes in common I ever heard about, so I know what it'll be like.
Girl: Well, I think you're silly. You'll be sorry when I tell you how funny it was.

[pause]

tone

[The recording is repeated.]

[pause]

Question 7   *Seven*
These people are talking about a colleague. What's his problem?
A   His boss is unfair to him.
B   He has been ill.
C   He has too much to do.

[pause]

tone

Man: I don't know what Jim's got to grumble about. My workload has doubled in the past year and I still manage. He's not doing any different from when he arrived, as far as I can see.
Woman: Yeah, but he's not as energetic as you are. Well, no one is. But Mr Craddock doesn't tell me off when I get a bit behind, he's very understanding with me. But with Jim, he goes on and on.
Man: I haven't noticed it, but you're probably right. I wonder why he does it?

[pause]

tone

[The recording is repeated.]

[pause]

Question 8   *Eight*
Listen to this woman phoning a travel agent. What does she want to do?
A cancel her booking
B postpone her holiday
C change her destination

[pause]

tone

Woman: … on the fourth of June … Yes. Amsterdam, Holland … Now, my problem is, my brother's there, and he was supposed to be fixing accommodation for me but he has a problem with his work right now and he asked me to reserve it from here … Yeah, well what it is, I don't really want to spend my vacation going around the city alone. So I wanted to ask you whether it would cost a lot to alter the flight, say till later in the summer, when maybe he'll be freer, and we might even get to visit a few more places?

[pause]

tone

[The recording is repeated.]

[pause]

That's the end of Part One.
Now turn to Part Two.

PART 2   *You will hear an interview about sports facilities. For questions 9 to 18 fill in the answers on the questionnaire. You now have forty-five seconds in which to look at Part Two.*

[pause]

tone

Woman: Excuse me, I'm doing some research on behalf of the local Sports Committee. Would you mind answering a few questions?
Man: Well, if it won't take too long, OK.
Woman: Thanks. Um, first of all, are you a local resident?
Man: Well, more or less. It's just south of the ring road.
Woman: Oh, right, so I could put you down as 'in the suburbs'?
Man: Yes.
Woman: And are you a student, or …?
Man: I've just started work actually. I'm a librarian.
Woman: Oh, yes? And do you use the public swimming pool regularly?
Man: About once a week, I suppose, though it might be less in winter.
Woman: Right. And what do you think about the hours it opens? Should it be open later, for example?
Man: Yes, I think it should. I'd use it more often if I could go later in the evening, and I think some of my friends would too.
Woman: Uh-huh. How about the cost? Are the charges reasonable?

Man:	Well, I can afford them now I'm earning, but it's not cheap, and considering it's not particularly luxurious, I think they're a bit too high, really. Especially for school kids and families.
Woman:	Mm. So you think the facilities could be improved?
Man:	Yes, they definitely need modernising. Apart from the odd coat of paint, they haven't changed since I was a kid. When I was in Birmingham the other week I went to a pool there and I couldn't believe the difference.
Woman:	Is there anything in particular you'd like to see added?
Man:	There definitely aren't enough showers! Anyone can tell you that!
Woman:	Yes, they do! And um, do you think there are any other sports which should be catered for locally but which aren't at the moment?
Man:	Well, the sports centre is good, although it's not all that big, but like most towns you haven't really got access to anywhere for athletics unless you travel to somewhere really big. And that's no good for kids who want to train regularly.
Woman:	Yes, I agree. And there's no coaching available either, once they get beyond a certain level, is there? Anyway, we must get on. If there could be some modernisation to the pool, or other sports facilities could be improved, do you have any opinion about how that should be paid for?
Man:	Well, that's the problem, isn't it? Personally, I wouldn't mind paying a bit more tax, if it would actually get spent on the right things. But I'm young and single and I can afford to say that. Really I think the Sports Committee need to get local businesses involved. That's probably the only practical possibility.
Woman:	Right. And – I've nearly done – there've been suggestions that some groups should be able to use the pool without charge. Do you agree with this, and if so who should that be?
Man:	I visited Australia last year and I discovered that where I was staying, pensioners could get in for nothing. I think that's a really good idea. And long term it could save on doctor's bills, couldn't it?
Woman:	I suppose it might. Well thank you very much for your help.
Man:	That's OK. Bye.
Woman:	Goodbye ... Excuse me, I'm doing some research on behalf of the local Sports ...

[pause]

tone

Now you'll hear Part Two again.

[The recording is repeated.]

[pause]

That's the end of Part Two.
Now turn to Part Three.

PART 3　*You will hear five people talking to someone they have just met. For questions 19 to 23, choose which of the people A to F each speaker is talking to. Use the letters only once. There is one extra letter which you do not need to use. You now have 30 seconds in which to look at Part Three.*

[pause]

tone

First woman:	I've never done anything like this before, have you?
Second woman:	Er, no.
First woman:	I mean I always thought that organised tours meant bunches of foreigners buzzing around with cameras saying, 'If it's Wednesday this must be Copenhagen'. But with such a small number you don't really feel we're tourists in that sense, do you?

[pause]

Woman:	Come to join the madhouse? This is my little corner here, and I think you'll find you're just round here.
Man:	Oh, thanks.
Woman:	Now I expect you'll want a few minutes to sort your stuff out, then I'll take you round and show you where everything is. OK?
Man:	Yes. Thank you very much.

[pause]

First man:	Have you ever been on one of these before? My boss says it'll make all the difference. Well, I think she hopes it will! I'm hopeless at time management.
Second man:	Oh?
First man:	Quite posh sort of place this, isn't it? I suppose that's the chap who's going to tell us what to do. It'd better be good. It's costing our companies quite a bit to send us.
Second man:	Mm.

[pause]

First woman:	I do hope you're going to like it here. We were so glad when we heard it'd been sold. It's not nice being near an empty place for so long. We've always found people to be very friendly, and you know, we help each other out with little jobs around the place. You're not married, are you?
Second woman:	Er, well.
First woman:	Well, do drop round any time if you want a hand with anything, or you need to know where to go for anything.
Second woman:	Thanks.

[pause]

Man:	Well, that's about it really. I hope you'll find it suits you. As I said, any queries, just call me and I'll see what I can sort out.
Woman:	Thanks.
Man:	And if you do decide to use the little room as an office, just let me know and I'll get the bed out and I'll bring you a desk.
Woman:	Right, thanks.
Man:	Anyway, I expect you want to get your stuff sorted out, so if you just give me your cheque for the first month, I'll hand over your keys and leave you to it.

[pause]

tone

Now you'll hear Part Three again.

[The recording is repeated.]

[pause]

That's the end of Part Three.
Now turn to Part Four.

PART 4   *You will hear a discussion between Andy and Sharon about advertising their small business. For questions 24 to 30, decide which of the statements are true and which are false and write T for True or F for False in the box provided. You now have forty-five seconds in which to look at Part Four.*

[pause]

tone

Andy:	What was it you wanted to discuss, Sharon?
Sharon:	Well, it's this thing about advertising, Andy. I think we need to get information about ourselves across to possible customers, otherwise we're just not going to increase sales.
Andy:	OK. We both accept we're going to have to spend more in order to get business. So, let's look at the situation. We've already paid out quite a bit for that advertisement in *Local Business News*. Everyone says it was a great little advertisement, they all like it when we show it to them. Do you think it was worth it?
Sharon:	That's the problem. We don't really know. But I suspect not. Because we need to reach the guys working in the offices, staff, whatever, and that magazine lies about in reception areas for bored customers.
Andy:	Yeah, I'm sure you're right. The woman who persuaded us to take that ad out was just after what she could get. We shouldn't have listened to her. What I think we should do is advertise in the local paper.
Sharon:	Oh, come on Andy, that rag!
Andy:	Yeah, I rang them and we thought that on the same page as jobs are advertised, under Business Services. So people who're, you know, just flicking through to see if there are any better jobs going, you know, everyone does it, they see this little ad, and think, Yeah, that'd be handy for us.
Sharon:	OK. Could we afford it every day?
Andy:	I thought every Thursday. That's when the most job adverts are in. They said they'd give quite a good discount if we have a long series, say for a few months.
Sharon:	Right, that's good. Anything else? I mean, what if we got some leaflets printed and stuck them through letterboxes?
Andy:	It could be very effective, but I think there's one big disadvantage.
Sharon:	Oh?
Andy:	Well, it'd take ages to deliver them all. We've got little enough time as it is.
Sharon:	But if we paid someone else to do it?
Andy:	Who, for example? It'd be too small scale for them to want to do. Anyway, we couldn't afford a professional firm.
Sharon:	Yeah, well, I'm not so sure of that. But anyway, what about getting some students to do it? It'd be a great way for them to earn a bit of money.
Andy:	Yeah, and I know just what'd happen. They'd stick the whole lot through the first five doors and push off home. We'd never be able to keep a check on them.
Sharon:	Oh, I don't know. Well, perhaps you're right. OK, let's look at the figures for the newspaper and then see whether we could afford anything else.

[pause]

tone

Now you'll hear Part Four again.

[The recording is repeated.]

[pause]

That is the end of Part Four.
There'll now be a pause of five minutes for you to copy your answers onto the separate answer sheet.
I'll remind you when there's one minute left, so that you're sure to finish in time.

[pause]

You have one more minute left.

[pause]

That's the end of the test. Please stop now. Your supervisor will now collect all the question papers and answer sheets.
Goodbye.

Book 1 Test 3 Key

Paper 1 Reading

Part 1
1 E   2 G   3 C   4 H   5 A   6 F   7 B

Part 2
8 C   9 D   10 A   11 C   12 B   13 A   14 C   15 B

Part 3
16 G   17 D   18 A   19 C   20 B   21 F

Part 4
22 and 23 A/B   24 D   **25 and 26** A/D   27 B   28 C
29 and 30 A/C   31 A   32 A   33 C   34 B   35 A
(Where there are two possible answers, these are interchangeable.)

Paper 3 Use of English

Award one mark for each correct answer, except in Part 3, where two marks are available, divided up as shown, for each answer.
    Correct spelling is essential throughout. Ignore omission or abuse of capital letters. No half marks.

Part 1
1 C   2 B   3 B   4 C   5 A   6 B   7 D   8 B   9 A
10 C   11 A   12 D   13 B   14 A   15 C

Part 2
16 to   17 an/the   18 make   19 with/under/in   20 what
21 at   22 as   23 while/when/if   24 both   25 but/whereas
26 is   27 this   28 than   29 not   30 can

Part 3
31 isn't/'s/is not worth (1) asking (1)
32 would not/wouldn't/did not/didn't let/refused to let (1) him buy/get (1)
33 where she had left (1) her (1)
34 way (1) John behaved (1)
35 if you (1) had not/hadn't lent (1)
36 no notice (1) of his doctor's (1)
37 in addition (1) to writing (1)
38 during/of (1) his childhood (1)

39 don't we/not (1) go to/go and visit (1)
40 had difficulty (in) (1) concentrating on (1)

Part 4

41 a   42 ✓   43 near   44 one   45 they   46 ✓   47 the
48 away   49 about   50 since   51 in   52 an   53 ✓
54 no   55 much

Part 5

56 width   57 height   58 disagreement   59 pressure
60 popularity   61 Unfortunately   62 wonderful   63 requirements
64 inhabitants   65 rarely

Paper 4 Listening

Part 1

1 A   2 A   3 A   4 B   5 A   6 C   7 C   8 B

Part 2

9 Thursday(s)   10 gallery   11 photography   12 print technology
13 model making   14 academic secretary   15 third year
16 stationery/notebooks   17 administration assistant   18 Department Head

Part 3

19 D   20 A   21 E   22 C   23 B

Part 4

24 C   25 A   26 B   27 B   28 A   29 C   30 B

Transcript   *First Certificate Practice Test Three. Paper Four. Listening. Hello, I'm going to give you the instructions for this test. I'll introduce each part of the test and give you time to look at the questions. At the start of each piece, you'll hear this sound:*

tone

You'll hear each piece twice.
Remember, while you're listening, write your answers on the question paper. You'll have time at the end of the test to copy your answers onto the separate answer sheet.
The tape will now be stopped. Please ask any questions now, because you must not speak during the test.

[pause]

PART 1 *Now, open your question paper and look at Part One. You'll hear people talking in eight different situations. For questions 1 to 8, choose the best answer, A, B or C.*

Question 1   One
You are visiting a trade exhibition when you hear a speaker at one of the stands. What is he demonstrating?
A *a watch*
B *a lock*
C *a burglar alarm*

[pause]

tone

Salesman: … and now I do up the strap, see, it clicks in and it's securely held. That won't slip, whatever you do, and as I said, you can't really damage it. Water's no problem, and if you leave if off and someone else tries to walk off with it, he'll soon regret it because of the high-pitched whistle which only you can de-activate …

[pause]

tone

[The recording is repeated.]

[pause]

Question 2   Two
This girl is talking about a party. What was it like?
A *boring*
B *too crowded*
C *noisy*

[pause]

tone

Girl: No, I wouldn't bother. The last one was useless. She'd made all this food, like she was expecting about fifty people, and then hardly anyone turned up, and her music system is useless, so unless you were next to it, you practically couldn't hear the music well enough to dance even though it was turned right up. It was dead dull, basically.

[pause]

tone

[The recording is repeated.]

[pause]

Question 3   Three
Listen to this hotel receptionist talking on the phone. Who is she talking to?
A *a friend*
B *a guest*
C *her employer*

[pause]

tone

Hotel receptionist: ... row about eleven o'clock. So old George went on up, thinking it was a burglar, and he was going to march him off ... Anyway it was this Mr Hardiman, he'd locked himself out and he was trying to force the door! You should've seen George's face ... That's right. And all the heads popping round their doors. Were we grateful the boss was away for the night!

[pause]

tone

[The recording is repeated.]

[pause]

Question 4 *Four*
You hear this advertisement on the radio. Who is it aimed at?
A people who have plenty of money
B people who might borrow money
C people who need to save money

[pause]

tone

Woman: Close your eyes and picture yourself in a beautiful dining-room. The table is dark wood, polished to a deep shine. The silver and glassware are reflected in the beautiful mirror hanging above the sideboard. Long curtains in rich brocade frame the window. Now, open your eyes and look around you. Fancy a change? It could all be yours with a loan from Home Finance Services. Just ring 0800 2323, that's 0800 2323 for details of our very competitive rates.

[pause]

tone

[The recording is repeated.]

[pause]

Question 5 *Five*
Listen to these students talking about their holiday work. Where are they working?
A a library
B an office
C a shop

[pause]

tone

Student 1: ... so then he just came up to me and said, 'Isn't it time you knew how to classify reference books?' He can be really mean.

Student 2: I know, and he makes you do the evenings when there's no one else there so you can't really stop people taking things out which aren't for external loans, and then he blames you because things are missing.

Student 1: So, I said, 'But at least I understand how the computer works!'

Student 2: I bet that got him.

Student 1: Yeah. He went all red and didn't speak to me for hours.

[pause]

tone

[The recording is repeated.]

[pause]

Question 6 *Six*
Listen to this man. Where has he been?
A to the gym
B to the dentist
C to the barber

[pause]

tone

Man: Just don't ask! It was the usual story. You go in and say, 'Look, I just want a trim, tidy up a few straggly ends'. You know. Next thing you know you're imprisoned in this chair while some madman is let loose on you and you end up looking like this! No, it's not funny.

[pause]

tone

[The recording is repeated.]

[pause]

Question 7 *Seven*
You hear this woman talking on the radio. What is she discussing?
A music
B a picture
C architecture

[pause]

tone

Woman: … I've got nothing against simple forms. Some of the most dramatic views in the world are created by a harmonious arrangement of very simple forms. That's fine. But this, this isn't simplicity, it's, it's flatness. It's painted in the dullest shades which are quite inappropriate to this climate. It's out of tune with its surroundings, and worst of all, I suspect, it will be unpleasant to work in as well as being an eyesore for people who have to pass by it every day.

[pause]

tone

[The recording is repeated.]

[pause]

Question 8   *Eight*
You hear this man talking to a shop assistant. Why is he annoyed?
A His pen has leaked in his pocket.
B His pen has been repaired recently.
C His pen was very expensive.

[pause]

tone

Man: Look, I realise it's not exactly the top of the range – it wasn't particularly expensive or anything, but you had it in for a repair only a fortnight ago and that cost far more than it should have done and then yesterday it started leaking when I was using it and made the most incredible mess. If it had done that in my pocket, it could have ruined an expensive suit. It really isn't on, you know!

[pause]

tone

[The recording is repeated.]

[pause]

That's the end of Part One.
Now turn to Part Two.

PART 2   *You will hear a teacher telling new students about their course. For questions 9 to 18 listen to what she says and complete the notes. You now have thirty seconds in which to look at Part Two.*

[pause]

tone

Teacher: Well, I'm very glad to welcome you all to the practical module of our Design course at the beginning of a new year. As you've no doubt realised, we have people here from years one to three, and we find that as most of the work is in small groups or individually-based, this works out pretty well, even though we're a bit short of space. Now I'm going to go through some administrative stuff and then we'll get on to project planning. So, first of all, hm, we're in the Studio here every afternoon except one, so we do have a sort of base, which is quite nice, but once a week we have to move out, that's into Room 51, which is on Thursdays. It's a bit of a nuisance, because it's not as big as in here, but we manage somehow. And on Fridays you can use the big space over the back of the hall, which is called the Gallery, for private study if you want to spread out a bit. That's only on Fridays though, I'm afraid. Now as far as extra courses go. You should've already selected these, and the days for them are as follows: um, Mondays is the only day when the darkroom is free, so that's photography. Tuesdays John Howard comes in here to take the sessions on Print Technology, and

Wednesdays I'm here for Model-making. Now if you haven't selected your options for this term, you need to get a move on. When we finish now, I'll be showing you round the rest of the department and you can get a form from the academic secretary on the way. Oh, you also need to get one if you want to do the full-day course, which is on Saturdays on Computer-aided Design. But that only applies to you third-year students, of course, and you know where the office is.

Now, that's nearly all, except a reminder to you all that we provide all the equipment you need for practical work, including card and photographic papers, but you must bring your own stationery. You should have proper notebooks, and we don't expect to have to find bits of paper for you to make notes on when you forget them. And, lastly, about absence. If you're not well, if it's just a couple of days, you can phone the administration assistant, ask him to pass a message on to this department. If it's more than a couple of days, you must send a written explanation to the Department Head otherwise you could be penalised in your course grade for absence without permission. OK? Well you have been warned. Now, for you new guys, let's go and look round the rest of the place. The rest of you no doubt have things to be getting on with.

[pause]

tone

Now you'll hear Part Two again.

[The recording is repeated.]

[pause]

That's the end of Part Two.
Now turn to Part Three.

PART 3 *You will hear five people saying thank you. For questions 19 to 23, choose which of A to F each speaker is talking about. Use the letters only once. There is one extra letter which you do not need to use. You now have 30 seconds in which to look at Part Three.*

[pause]

tone

Man: This is not an occasion where it is easy for me to know what to say. I realised of course that I wouldn't get away without some kind of little memento. After all, we've been together a long time and I know what a generous bunch you are. But I had absolutely no idea that it was going to be something like this. It's quite magnificent. Really, I'm lost for words. Except that I'm beginning to think I'll have to move house. It's so grand it'll make the rest of the place look terrible in comparison! Thank you all very, very much.

[pause]

Woman: I just called to say thank you. I've just had my results. And I know I'd never have done so well if you hadn't been pushing me this last term! ... Well, it's nice of you to say so, but honestly, I never even found the subject interesting until I got into your class.

[pause]

Man: Anyway, thanks very much for putting me on to them. They were just the right people for the job. I don't know why nobody here had heard of them. But as the boss says, 'If you want to know anything about anything, all you have to do is ask Carole! She's got all the answers.' Many thanks, and let me know if ever I can help you out some way.

[pause]

Man: Well, I certainly owe you one this time. Thank you very much indeed for telling me what might happen. It would have been a total disaster if I'd let them take it away. I think you've just saved me a lot of money. And listen, if I can do anything for you, all you have to do is name it!

[pause]

Woman: I'd like to take this opportunity to thank all of you for your hard work over the past few months. I don't need to tell you but, er, I want you to be sure that I know too, that without you guys here doing all the routine, and not so routine, work, and doing it without much understanding from outside, so that I could get on with my stuff – well, I wouldn't have achieved anything. It was a tough job for all of us and I won't forget what you've all done for me, I promise.

[pause]

tone

Now you'll hear Part Three again.

[The recording is repeated.]

[pause]

That's the end of Part Three.
Now turn to Part Four.

PART 4   *You will hear a radio discussion about a wildlife park. For questions 24 to 30, decide which of the choices, A, B or C is the correct answer. You now have one minute in which to look at Part Four.*

[pause]

tone

Gary: Now, I have with me here this evening two people who are both very interested in the future of Glenside Park. Helen, you represent the management committee of the park, and Ian (Good evening.), you represent the residents of the village of South Glen which lies just beyond the park and through which the main road into the park passes. I understand that the residents aren't too happy about some of your plans, Helen. Could you just give us an outline of what exactly these are?

Helen: Well, yes, I'm very happy to explain because I think part of the problem that has arisen is that some people in South Glen have got the wrong idea about our plans. Once they see what we're trying to do here, I think they'll agree it's a very sensible way forward.

Ian: We see perfectly well, we just don't happen to think you're right ...

Gary: OK, Ian, Ian, you'll have your say in a minute. Now, Helen, what exactly is it you're proposing?

Helen: Yes. As you know, Glenside has two problems at the moment. First, we're short of money, and second we've got too many people wandering about in parts of the park where animals, especially the birds, are trying to raise their young, disturbing them and sometimes causing the young to be left by their parents, so the staff have to try and save them by raising them by hand, which takes up precious time and, of course, is expensive.

Gary: So what do you want to do?

Helen: We think the best way to raise money would be to have more visitors to the park who'd be prepared to pay to see the animals.

Ian: But that's ridiculous! (No, it's not.) On the one hand you're accusing people of upsetting the animals, and then the next minute you're saying you want more people wandering about.

Helen: No, the point is that at the moment, people walk all over the place, they don't keep to the roads, they scare the birds, and there's a constant danger that a fire might be started and we wouldn't be able to do anything because we wouldn't know until it was too late.

Ian: Wait a minute, wait a minute. What are you talking about? People from the village would no more want to damage the park than you do!

Helen: I don't mean they'd do it on purpose. But there are such things as accidents.

Ian: Oh, come on – how many fires have you had in the last ten years?

Helen: I'm not saying we have, just that we might. Now, what we want is to have fixed routes through the park, so that visitors can be taken through and have things pointed out and explained ...

Ian: And where might these people park, may one enquire? Because it won't help relations with the village if all the roads through it are blocked with tourist cars and buses and we can't even walk through the woods where our parents and grandparents have been able to walk for generations, without paying for the honour!

Gary: He has got a point there, I think, Helen. After all, it would be quite a revolutionary plan, wouldn't it?

Helen: But people can't expect something for nothing. No, they could get tickets for a season, so they wouldn't have to queue. But they'd have to learn to respect the wildlife.

Ian: Look, tell me one example of serious harm which has been done by a local resident. We've been here for years before you turned up. If we didn't respect the land and the living things on it, it wouldn't be here for people like you to move in and start making profits out of. What have you ever done for South Glen?

Gary: OK, OK, OK, well, well, I can see that we're going to have a lot more discussion about this before the plans are carried out. (Yeah.) There is going to be a public meeting next Wednesday at South Glen Community Centre and I'm sure it'll be well-attended. Now, I think perhaps we need some music to calm us down, so here's a little tune I'm sure ...

[pause]

tone

Now you'll hear Part Four again.

[The recording is repeated.]

[pause]

That is the end of Part Four.
There'll now be a pause of five minutes for you to copy your answers onto the separate answer sheet.

I'll remind you when there's one minute left, so that you're sure to finish in time.

[pause]

You have one more minute left.

[pause]

That's the end of the test. Please stop now. Your supervisor will now collect all the question papers and answer sheets.
Goodbye.

Book 1 Test 4 Key

Paper 1 Reading

Part 1
1 D   2 F   3 A   4 H   5 B   6 G   7 E

Part 2
8 D   9 D   10 A   11 A   12 B   13 C   14 B

Part 3
15 E   16 F   17 B   18 G   19 C   20 H   21 A

Part 4
22 and 23 A/C   24 D   25 C   26 B   27 A   28 and 29 B/D
30 A   31 D   32 A   33 and 34 B/D   35 E
(Where there are two possible answers, these are interchangeable.)

Paper 3 Use of English

Award one mark for each correct answer, except in Part 3, where two marks are available, divided up as shown, for each answer.
    Correct spelling is essential throughout. Ignore omission or abuse of capital letters. No half marks.

Part 1
1 C   2 D   3 B   4 B   5 D   6 A   7 C   8 B   9 A
10 D   11 C   12 B   13 D   14 C   15 B

Part 2
16 another *(allow* each/every); [*not* a]   17 of   18 a   19 it
20 for   21 who   22 became [*not* was]   23 would   24 By
25 have   26 may/might   27 which/that   28 capable
29 Until/Till   30 in

Part 3
31 (that) Brenda (1) waited/(should) wait (1)
    or to Brenda (1) she should wait/(that) she wait(ed); [Brenda to wait = 0]
32 not (1) waking/getting up (1)
33 first time (1) I have/I've eaten (1)
34 managed (1) to arrest (1)
35 ought to have (1) written (1)
36 has (1) such small handwriting (that) (1)

37 have to/must (1) be picked up (1)
38 regret telling him (1) our plans (1)
39 everyone's surprise (,) (1) Geoff left (1)
40 I was to blame (1) for (1)

Part 4

41 ✓   42 still   43 so   44 a   45 ✓   46 as   47 the
48 when   49 for   50 it   51 also   52 ✓   53 well
54 ourselves   55 ✓

Part 5

56 speaking   57 preparation   58 encouraged   59 ensure
60 correctly   61 liking   62 tastiest   63 dangerous
64 importance   65 heavily

Paper 4 Listening

Part 1

1 A   2 C   3 A   4 C   5 B   6 A   7 A   8 B

Part 2

9 (beautiful, sandy) beach   10 medium-sized   11 drive/car
12 June   13 (enormous) cliffs   14 tiny   15 coach   16 model village
17 drive/car   18 winter

Part 3

19 D   20 A   21 E   22 B   23 C

Part 4

24 A   25 C   26 C   27 A   28 C   29 S   30 S

Transcript   *First Certificate Practice Test Four. Paper Four. Listening. Hello, I'm going to give you the instructions for this test. I'll introduce each part of the test and give you time to look at the questions. At the start of each piece, you'll hear this sound.*

tone

You'll hear each piece twice.
Remember, while you're listening, write your answers on the question paper. You'll have time at the end of the test to copy your answers onto the separate answer sheet.
The tape will now be stopped. Please ask any questions now, because you must not speak during the test.

[pause]

PART 1   *Now open your question paper and look at Part One.*
You'll hear people talking in eight different situations. For questions 1 to 8,
choose the best answer, A, B or C.

Question 1   One
These women are talking about a colleague. What do they feel about his
behaviour?
A It was typical of him.
B It had improved.
C It reminded them of someone else.

[pause]

tone

First woman: Well, it was hardly surprising really, was it? D'you remember how he went on when we tried to change the booking system?

Second woman: You'd have thought he'd invented it himself the way he was carrying on.

First woman: This time he went right to the Section Manager. He's a real pain about that sort of thing.

Second woman: He doesn't seem to be able to see that we're only trying to make things work better.

First woman: Exactly. I just can't get through to him at all.

[pause]

tone

[The recording is repeated.]

[pause]

Question 2   Two
This man is talking about a sports event. What happened to his team?
A They won.
B They did better than he'd hoped.
C They were very unlucky.

[pause]

tone

Man: It was incredible! We'd come right up through the league from the qualifying round. I'd always known we'd had it in us if we could just get it together. And we'd been really lucky when Mike moved into the area and joined us. It made a lot of difference. And then, there we were all set for the final, everyone in top form and three men had to pull out for silly little reasons. I couldn't believe my ears when they phoned, one after another. From then on, I knew what to expect. Even the winners said luck had been on their side.

[pause]

tone

[The recording is repeated.]

[pause]

Question 3   *Three*
           Listen to this man telephoning someone about his washing machine. Who is
           he talking to?
           A an engineer
           B a friend
           C the shop he bought it from

           [pause]

           tone

Man: … been in touch with them already and they said it's not up to them, because the
           guarantee doesn't cover it. So I was wondering whether it might be the sort of thing you
           could handle? … I don't suppose you could give me any idea of what the charge might
           be? … Yes, I see. The thing is, I've got some friends coming round this weekend and
           um … Oh, that'd be great!

           [pause]

           tone

           [The recording is repeated.]

           [pause]

Question 4   *Four*
           You switch on the radio and hear this report. Where is it coming from?
           A a market
           B a concert hall
           C a racetrack

           [pause]

           tone

Sports reporter: And there's a tremendous crowd here today – everyone's milling about, looking very
           excited. There's laughter and music and lots of chatter. I've been talking to some of the
           people around me and there's no doubt that there's a fair amount of money changing
           hands as well. And now we'll go over to Arnold Burns who's been watching the runners
           coming up to the start.

           [pause]

           tone

           [The recording is repeated.]

           [pause]

Question 5   *Five*
           You hear this man talking about his bad back. How did he injure it?
           A in a road accident
           B by lifting something
           C in a fight

           [pause]

tone

Man: It's not much better. Thanks for asking. I wouldn't mind so much if I hadn't been trying to help someone else. You know, John was there, struggling with this damn great case and I thought, oh, I can't leave him to cope on his own, so I went over and said, 'Let's get it up onto the wheels', and I was sort of lifting, and he was pushing, and suddenly I just felt something go in my back and that was it.

[pause]

tone

[The recording is repeated.]

[pause]

Question 6 *Six*
You overhear these people talking about a book. What sort of book is it?
A *a guidebook*
B *a history book*
C *a novel*

[pause]

tone

Man: ... so I asked him what he thought, 'cause he'd been there.
Woman: And so?
Man: Well, he said most of the descriptions were quite accurate. You know, the old bits of the town, they really do look like that even now. But the factual details about good value for money, he said, they're not really aimed at people like us.
Woman: How do you mean?
Man: Well, it's written for older people really, so what he says is reasonably cheap, is really quite expensive, and when he says some old inn or something is 'adequate', we'd find it really comfortable.
Woman: Perhaps I'd better see if I can find something more suitable.

[pause]

tone

[The recording is repeated.]

[pause]

Question 7 *Seven*
Listen to this woman who has just arrived at a meeting. Why is she late?
A *The weather was bad.*
B *There was a traffic jam.*
C *She crashed her car.*

[pause]

tone

Woman: I'm so sorry. I do hope you haven't been waiting to begin. It was just after I left Oxford, there was this tremendously heavy rain and all the traffic had to slow right down, you couldn't see a thing. I was convinced I was going to hit something. Anyway, I'm really sorry.

[pause]

tone

[The recording is repeated.]

[pause]

Question 8   *Eight*
At the sports club you hear these people discussing an exercise. What is its purpose?
A to help you lose weight
B to make you relax
C to strengthen the stomach muscles

[pause]

tone

Man:	So, was the class any use?
Woman:	It was pretty tiring! We did do some quite good things though. There was one where you had to lie on your stomach, and very gently move your arms from above your head down to your sides.
Man:	Hardly very energetic!
Woman:	But you feel very sort of calm afterwards. All the tension goes out of your shoulders. At least that's the idea, apparently.

[pause]

tone

[The recording is repeated.]

[pause]

That's the end of Part One.
Now turn to Part Two.

PART 2   *You will hear part of a radio programme about holidays. For questions 9 to 18, complete the grid. You now have thirty seconds in which to look at Part Two.*

[pause]

tone

Presenter:	Hello and welcome to the Holiday Spot. Today we have reports on three contrasting places, all within a couple of hours of the capital. And first we have Gabrielle, who's been to Eastingham.
Gabrielle:	Yes, well, I must admit I thought I was the unlucky one, getting Eastingham, but in fact I was really pleasantly surprised. I thought the main attraction would be night clubs and fast food bars. In fact it's just a medium-sized town with an old-fashioned sea front, and

most of the visitors are there for the absolutely beautiful sandy beach, which is actually more impressive in reality than on the postcards. I went by road, as it didn't occur to me that I could go by train, and I must say that although it might have saved me half an hour, it would have meant quite a long walk at the other end, as the station is on the inland side of the town. Also, for a day trip, a car's a must, as the last train is a very slow one. And I had no trouble parking even though I was there in August. I was told that June is ideal, when the weather is most likely to be sunshine but the crowds haven't got too bad. Actually I suspect that Eastingham's idea of really crowded would be some resorts' idea of pleasantly lively. Um, for a relaxed day in the traditional style, Eastingham's just the place.

Presenter: Thanks, Gabrielle. Now we turn to Josh, who's been sampling the delights of Brant, just ten miles along the coast.

Josh: Yes, I've just returned from an amazing weekend. Brant is a tiny place with several excellent homely guest houses and visitors come here because it's a great base for a walking holiday. Its most exciting feature is the enormous cliffs which rear up above the sea. It's not too difficult to reach from the city, only about an hour and half's drive by coach and these go most days. It's not really a good idea to take your own car, even though the roads aren't bad, because the parking space is very restricted and during the day it's expensive. But a great place to get the traffic fumes out of your lungs.

Presenter: Thank you Josh. You certainly sound refreshed. And lastly, we hear from Catherine, who's been on a day trip to Faresey. I believe you took some friends with you, Catherine?

Catherine: Well, I'd heard that Faresey boasted an attraction which was popular with children from eight to eighty, so I took my neighbour Tom, who's twelve, and his granddad, Alec, who's seventy. And, well, the day was a roaring success. Faresey is the home of a model railway, but what really pulls in the crowds is that you can spend hours going round an entire model village, complete with market, workshops and houses, all based on Faresey in the nineteenth century. I was fascinated by it, and so were my friends. I had been worried that there wouldn't be enough to keep Tom occupied, but the working model machines really hooked him. Faresey itself is a pleasant small town, and the model village is something which you can't help being interested by. It's easy to get to if you drive, as it's just ten minutes from the motorway, about forty minutes altogether from here. And it's open all the year round. In fact, I'd recommend it as a good day out during winter rather than summer, as you could still be there and back in daylight and the crowds might be thinner, so you wouldn't have to wait for a clear view of the models. Not that that's a great problem, even in summer, but you do have to be a bit patient at some of the best bits.

Presenter: Well, it sounds as though you've all had a good time. Many thanks. And now to our foreign holiday slot. Here's Jenny …

[pause]

tone

Now you'll hear Part Two again.

[The recording is repeated.]

[pause]

That's the end of Part Two.
Now turn to Part Three.

PART 3   *You will hear five people talking about clothes. For questions 19 to 23, choose from the list A to F what each speaker is talking about. Use the letters only once. There is one extra letter which you do not need to use. You now have 30 seconds in which to look at Part Three.*

[pause]

tone

Woman: And now here is Patrick. This is beautifully cut in fine wool with hand-sewn detail on the sleeves and a flattering pleat at the waistline of the trousers. The jacket lining is of silk, making it wonderfully comfortable. This is an absolute must for winter which you'll still be wearing next spring. It's available in a range of colours, both classic and more adventurous.

[pause]

Woman: I've had it for years. Actually I think it was my grandfather's. I expect he used to wear it on expeditions. It keeps the sun out of your eyes without making your head hot. Everyone laughs at illustrations of nineteenth-century costume, but all the same they did get some things right. And this is one of them. Well, as far as I'm concerned anyway.

[pause]

Man: Well, it was pouring with rain, as you know, and when we got there I had to take my shoes off because they were absolutely soaked. It was so embarrassing. There was this great hole with my toe sticking out. I'm sure it wasn't there when I was getting dressed. It must have caught on the shoe lining and then just spread. Well, what could I do? I just laughed!

[pause]

Woman: Where does he find them? Last week he had on, I'm not joking, an open-necked, orange and pink nylon striped one. He looked like a garden chair. Jeremy said it gave him a headache looking at it all day. I don't know what the customers make of it. You'd think he'd get cold in those short sleeves too.

[pause]

Man: Yeah, I'm very pleased with it really. It's big enough to go over anything, it's really warm and it looks smart enough. I never used to bother when I drove to work, but now I'm using the train I needed something to keep out the wind and rain. That's why I have it so long. It keeps my knees dry too.

[pause]

tone

Now you'll hear Part Three again.

[The recording is repeated.]

[pause]

That's the end of Part Three.
Now turn to Part Four.

PART 4　*You will hear two friends discussing evening study courses. For questions 24 to 30, decide which course each statement refers to. Mark A for Art, or C for Computers or S for Spanish. You now have forty-five seconds in which to look at Part Four.*

[pause]

tone

Tracy:　Hey, Polly, how's it going?

Polly:　Hi, Tracy. Hey, I went into the Institute on my way home today to find out about evening classes. They've got some very good courses planned this year.

Tracy:　Oh, did you get a leaflet?

Polly:　No, they're re-printing them. But some are the same as last year, and I made a couple of notes.

Tracy:　I'm not sure I really want to bother this year. It's such a drag turning out again after you get in in the evening. And that painting course had so many people in it that you couldn't really get any individual help.

Polly:　Yes, well they've decided to limit the numbers this year, so if you want to do it you have to book a place. I can understand why, I suppose. Anyway I don't know, but I wonder whether I ought to do the computing really. It might be useful. I mean if I was going for promotion.

Tracy:　But would it be advanced enough for you, Polly? You already do quite a lot of that sort of thing, don't you?

Polly:　Oh, I think so. The woman who runs it is supposed to be very good. She's not just a programmer, she's a trained teacher as well.

Tracy:　Well, it's up to you of course. Sounds like my idea of hell, at the end of a day's work. I just want something relaxing.

Polly:　But Tracy, I think you really ought to do something, even if it's just the same one as last year.

Tracy:　But then I'd have to pay for materials. That's another reason I don't think I want to do it again. I can't afford more than the minimum.

Polly:　Well, why don't you try Spanish? It'd be easy for you, Tracy, knowing Italian, and it'd be really useful on holiday.

Tracy:　Mm. Don't the language courses last two terms? I don't know I want to tie myself up for that long.

Polly:　Er, I don't think so, no. That's the computer course. But they're pretty intensive so you really get through a lot in a short time.

Tracy:　If it's so good, why don't you try it yourself?

Polly:　I'd like to, it's just I ought to consider my career and I don't have time for both.

Tracy:　Oh, well. Let's think about it over the weekend.

Polly:　All right.

[pause]

tone

Now you'll hear Part Four again.

[The recording is repeated.]

[pause]

That is the end of Part Four.
There'll now be a pause of five minutes for you to copy your answers onto the separate answer sheet.
I'll remind you when there's one minute left, so that you're sure to finish in time.

[pause]

You have one more minute left.

[pause]

That's the end of the test. Please stop now. Your supervisor will now collect all the question papers and answer sheets. Goodbye.

Book 2 Test 1 Key

Paper 1 Reading

Part 1
1 F   2 G   3 A   4 D   5 C   6 E

Part 2
7 C   8 A   9 B   10 D   11 B   12 A   13 C   14 D

Part 3
15 D   16 A   17 G   18 C   19 F   20 B

Part 4
21 B   22 D   23 and 24 B/E   25 B   26 E   27 A   28 C
29 B   30 D   31 B   32 A   33 E   34 A   35 C
(Where there are two possible answers, these are interchangeable.)

Paper 3 Use of English

Award one mark for each correct answer, except in Part 3, where two marks are available, divided up as shown, for each answer.

Correct spelling is essential throughout. Ignore omission or abuse of capital letters. No half marks.

Part 1
1 B   2 D   3 A   4 B   5 C   6 D   7 A   8 B   9 C
10 A   11 A   12 C   13 D   14 A   15 B

Part 2
16 all   17 where   18 answer/reply   19 happened/occurred
20 someone/somebody   21 so   22 which/that   23 for/about
24 be/prove   25 one/theirs   26 case   27 of   28 try
29 what   30 yourself

Part 3
31 told us/given/explained the OR given (us) a (1) reason for (1)
32 prefer you (1) not to phone (1)
33 took Mary (1) a year to (1)
34 is being/will be released (1) from (1)
35 if/whether he (1) had left (1)
36 went in (1) for (1)
37 have no intention (1) of telling (1)

38 missing (1) before you (1)
39 Sasha wouldn't (1) have moved (1)
40 has to (1) be cleaned (1)

Part 4

41 it   42 by   43 the   44 ✓   45 so   46 their   47 ✓
48 up   49 being   50 then   51 since   52 had   53 a
54 for   55 ✓

Part 5

56 elsewhere   57 Naturally   58 convenience   59 actors/actresses
60 scientific   61 researchers   62 actually   63 designed
64 unlike   65 appearance

Paper 4 Listening

Part 1

1 A   2 B   3 C   4 C   5 B   6 A   7 C   8 A

Part 2

9 early career   10 (mystery) host   11 (the) Far East
12 (a) student(s)   13 (student) travelcards
14 rock musicians/big (music) names   15 Jamaica
16 trip to Brazil   17 (a) shoe museum   18 dancing (in clubs)/to clubs

Part 3

19 C   20 A   21 D   22 B   23 F

Part 4

24 S   25 F   26 M   27 F   28 S   29 F   30 S

Transcript   *First Certificate Practice Test One. Paper Four. Listening. Hello. I'm going to give you the instructions for this test. I'll introduce each part of the test and give you time to look at the questions.*
At the start of each piece, you'll hear this sound:

tone

You'll hear each piece twice.
Remember, while you're listening, write your answers on the question paper. You'll have time at the end of the test to copy your answers onto the separate answer sheet.

The tape will now be stopped. Please ask any questions now, because you must not speak during the test.

[pause]

PART 1 *Now open your question paper and look at Part One.*
You'll hear people talking in eight different situations. For questions 1 to 8, choose the best answer, A, B or C.

Question 1 *One*
You hear someone introducing a programme on the radio. Where is he?
A a swimming-pool
B a sports hall
C a football ground

[pause]

tone

Reporter: . . . and I'm here outside now and there's quite a crowd beginning to build up behind the fence. They're hoping to get in to see what the new changing rooms are like – supposed to be really luxurious compared to the old ones – and also the new diving area which I understand is overlooked by the café – should make that a good place to pass the time while you're getting dry. And now here is the Mayor of Taunton arriving to actually perform the opening ceremony . . .

[pause]

tone

[The recording is repeated.]

[pause]

Question 2 *Two*
You hear this girl talking to her mother. Which plan had her mother accepted?
A visiting a friend
B going to London
C staying in a hotel

[pause]

tone

Girl: But you said it was all right.
Mother: That was for the day. You're not wandering about London at night, staying with some friends of Antonia's brother I've never heard of . . .
Girl: We could stay in a hotel.
Mother: That shows just how little you and Antonia know about it. I agreed to a day's shopping and so did her mother. Either you come back on the evening train or you don't go.
Girl: Oh, Mum.

[pause]

tone

[The recording is repeated.]

[pause]

Question 3   *Three*
You hear this advertisement for a concert. What is unusual about it?
A It's on a Saturday.
B It's in a different place.
C There will be singers in it.

[pause]

tone

Announcer: Next Saturday evening the City Symphony Orchestra will be joined for their regular monthly concert, starting at eight o'clock, at the Festival Hall, by singers from the High School and the City Music Society, for a performance of Beethoven's Ninth Symphony. An occasion not to be missed, I'm sure.

[pause]

tone

[The recording is repeated.]

[pause]

Question 4   *Four*
You hear this woman talking about herself. What does she feel?
A regret
B pride
C satisfaction

[pause]

tone

Woman: I think it's very difficult for people nowadays to imagine how it was for us. We had far fewer choices than girls nowadays. I know I never married, and it wouldn't be true to say I never thought about the pleasures of bringing up children. But on the whole I don't think I'm suited to motherhood. So I've no doubt it was for the best. Anyway – the choice was partly my own and partly just the way things turned out for me – I really don't see any reason to complain.

[pause]

tone

[The recording is repeated.]

[pause]

Question 5   *Five*
Listen to this man on the phone. Why is he calling?
A to apologise for being late
B to report escaped animals
C to offer his help

[pause]

tone

Man: I'm actually on my way to town now . . . no, no, . . . sorry to be the bringer of bad news, but . . . yes, I came down the back road and they're all over the place . . . the hedge is all smashed up. Will you be able to fix something, do you think? . . . I'm really sorry, I just can't – I've got to get to my meeting . . . At least the bull wasn't in there with them! . . . Yeah, okay, I'll probably be round tonight. . . . Sure. See you later.

[pause]

tone

[The recording is repeated.]

[pause]

Question 6   *Six*
             You hear this reporter on the television. Who is he going to talk to?
             A a businessman
             B a politician
             C a shopper

[pause]

tone

Reporter: . . . for many years now. They say that the market is no longer needed, as people shop in the suburbs, and it just leads to worse traffic problems. But the fact remains that there's been a market on this spot for hundreds of years and a number of local shopkeepers feel that without it, the city centre will just die. They've got together to make their views known to the authorities. One of them's here with me now. Alan Green, what exactly is it you think should be done here?

[pause]

tone

[The recording is repeated.]

[pause]

Question 7   *Seven*
             This boy is talking about something he's been working on. What is it?
             A a garden
             B a water sports centre
             C a nature reserve

[pause]

tone

Teenage boy: We, er, started with just three of us, then I got some other people along, er, from, you know, school and things. We've cleaned up the litter from the grass banks, and fixed, like, a path, with markers, so people don't go too near where the birds nest. We've done a map of, um, the best places to, er, watch them from. There's a sailing club at the other end of the lake, but, er, they've said, we asked them, and they've said they're going to put markers across the water too. So, that'll be a big help.

[pause]

tone

[The recording is repeated.]

[pause]

Question 8   *Eight*
You hear this woman talking to someone outside a block of flats. What is her job?
A *She sells property.*
B *She is a tourist guide.*
C *She inspects building work.*

[pause]

tone

Estate agent: . . . as you can see, the outside of the block is maintained to a high standard, and the gardens are extremely well-designed. This block was built just under a hundred years ago and a number of well-known people have lived here, including poets, artists and writers. Now, if we go up to the flat I want to show you, you'll see that the view across to the castle is really something special. Now, as I mentioned on the phone, these are rarely available, so if you are interested I would advise you to let us know . . .

[pause]

tone

[The recording is repeated.]

[pause]

That's the end of Part One.
Now turn to Part Two.

PART 2   *You will hear two radio presenters talking about some of the programmes for the coming month. For questions 9 to 18, complete the information. You will need to write a word or a short phrase.*
You now have forty-five seconds in which to look at Part Two.

[pause]

tone

Rita: And now I've got with me Greg, who's going to fill us in on some of the special things coming up this month. What've you got for us, Greg?
Greg: Hi, Rita. Yeah, I've got several really special programmes to tell you about.
Rita: And this is retro month here on Intersound, so I guess we'll be looking back quite a bit?
Greg: That's right. And we start with an interview which'll take us back to the music scene in the early seventies – that's Elton John talking about his early career – and we'll be playing some of his favourite early tracks.

Rita: And that's on Monday the 6th?

Greg: At seven-thirty.

Rita: Great. And then on Wednesday the 8th we're going to visit somebody else connected with the seventies, am I right?

Greg: Yes, but I'm not telling you any more, because that's this month's mystery visit, when I talk to someone in their home and listeners have the chance to win a great prize by ringing in with their guesses as to the identity of my mystery host. Now all I'm going to say is that this is someone we associate with travelling at very high speed.

Rita: A sports personality, Greg?

Greg: You'll have to wait and find out after the show, Rita, like everyone else! That's from seven to eight.

Rita: OK, OK. Well, on Thursday we have our regular concert tour report. Who is it this week, Greg?

Greg: It's one of your favourite bands, Sez U, and we'll be reporting on their tour of the Far East.

Rita: Which was quite a rave –

Greg: Yeah. The report, with some great music, is at nine-thirty Thursday.

Rita: I shan't miss it. Now, what about Student Scene this month?

Greg: Right, well we've got a special feature on what it's like to be a university student in the States. That'll be specially interesting to anyone thinking about doing some studying over there, I guess. That's on Friday the 17th at 4 p.m. Then on Monday the 20th at the same time, I shall be looking at how to get the best out of student travelcards, how to get around Europe for as little money as possible.

Rita: Sounds like useful stuff. And what about the retro theme? Are there any other features later on in the month which take us back?

Greg: Yeah, we're putting together a programme about people whose parents were big music names of the sixties and seventies, asking them what it was like to grow up with parents who'd many of them broken all the rules themselves.

Rita: Pretty hard to shock them, I guess.

Greg: Well, I think you're in for some surprises. Apparently, rock musicians can be surprisingly strict parents! Find out on Friday the 24th at five o'clock.

Rita: Right. What else?

Greg: On Monday the 27th at one o'clock, we've got an hour for reggae fans, when we feature the sound of Jamaica thirty years back. And the same evening, we've got a special competition, which is going to win someone an all expenses paid trip to Brazil. Can you imagine it?

Rita: Wow! What time?

Greg: The questions will be put out at nine, one, and seven. So everyone will have a chance to hear them.

Rita: Don't miss it, you guys. And I think our time's just about up, Greg, but I just want to mention a couple of fashion notes you've missed at the end of the month. First, on the 28th, I'll be visiting a shoe museum and talking to Anna Trent, the curator, to find out whether our modern shoe fashions are as new as we think they are. And on the 29th, I'll be visiting some of Manchester's top clubs to report on a revolution in style amongst dancers on the club scene. Want to come?

Greg: You bet you. And now we'd better get on with the music, hadn't we?

Rita: Yup. And . . .

[pause]

tone

Now you'll hear Part Two again.

[The recording is repeated.]

[pause]

That's the end of Part Two.
Now turn to Part Three.

PART 3 *You will hear five people talking about the jobs they'd like to have. For questions 19 to 23, choose from the list A to F what they describe. Use the letters only once. There is one extra letter which you do not need to use. You now have thirty seconds in which to look at Part Three.*

[pause]

tone

Woman: Yes, I've been, you know, thinking about getting back to work, now my children are at school all day. Um, I used to have a job, in the parks department at the council actually. It was very nice in some ways, you know, a nice atmosphere. I thought I might do um, some training, in planning people's um – like, what plants grow in different soils, and how to group them. I'd like going to meet them and discussing their – what they needed doing, you know, that sort of thing.

[pause]

Man: I want to do something that can make a difference to people. The trouble with this country is people don't really know what's going on. I mean, even things that affect, you know, their daily lives. So I could go out and really find out what's happening, meet the people who make the decisions and then produce articles that put the readers in the picture.

[pause]

Woman: I'm not afraid of hard work. I think some people go into, like, what do they call them, caring professions, thinking it's all about being kind and getting gratitude. Actually, I know it's actually quite, well, very, in fact sometimes, physically hard. And you have to study chemistry and biology and stuff. And sick people can be, well, you know, impatient, or depressed. But I still want to do it. I think if you can give, in your career, then you can't turn your back on it.

[pause]

Man: I'm very much what they call a 'people' person, so I'd like to feel I was one, um, part of a team, working to give the guests a good time, and I'd like to feel that I was perhaps their first contact as they came in, and I'm quite, you know, lively and smiley, I think. So that should help them to feel better, if they were worn out, you know, at the end of a long journey or something. And I think the leisure industry is growing, so that'd be good, career wise, I think.

[pause]

Man: I'm looking for something that will let me have contact with people. I've had several jobs in the past, mostly in offices, companies, sometimes quite interesting, but you're not dealing with the public. I'd like to be looking after people, not bits of paper. I think the sort of big store where people go to make, er, major purchases, furniture, you know, where the decisions will affect their lives for years, so you can really help them if you're well-informed about the products. I think that'd be quite rewarding, actually.

[pause]

tone

Now you'll hear Part Three again.

[The recording is repeated.]

[pause]

That's the end of Part Three.
Now turn to Part Four.

PART 4 *You will hear a conversation between a father, a mother and their son. For questions 24 to 30, decide who expresses each idea and mark F for the father, M for the mother and S for the son.*
You now have forty-five seconds in which to look at Part Four.

[pause]

tone

Son: Do you know the people at the house on the corner are building a swimming-pool in their garden?

Father: Yeah, the Rawlings. They got a lot of money when their grandfather sold his business.

Mother: Did they? I suppose you think they're wasting it.

Son: No, it'd be great. Just think of getting up in the morning and having a swim before breakfast.

Father: Ugh. Not in this climate. They'd be better off getting their roof fixed.

Mother: Oh, really. Don't be so sensible! But honestly, I don't know why they're bothering. If I could afford a swimming-pool, you wouldn't catch me sticking around here.

Son: What?

Father: But this is a very popular area. We were very lucky to get this house at a reasonable price.

Mother: Oh, it's very convenient, I know. But if you can afford to have a swimming-pool, you could live somewhere much nicer.

Father: Like where?

Son: By the sea, for example?

Mother: Or anywhere, well out of town. Somewhere with beautiful views. Up in the hills away from the traffic.

Father: But we wouldn't be able to get to work.

Son: She means, if we had so much money it didn't matter.

Father: Oh, I see. Oh, well – we can all dream, I suppose. I don't think even the Rawlings could afford to give up working. I wonder if we'll be asked round when they've finished it?

Mother: Not if they hear us saying they should've spent it on the roof. But it is a funny thing to do, really.

Son:	I expect they just want to make people envy them.
Father:	Yeah, they're either really concerned about what their neighbours think or –
Mother:	– they have absolutely no idea how much people talk in this sort of neighbourhood!
Son:	Yeah.
Mother:	Well, anyway, we'd better clear this table. Someone's got homework, I presume?
Son:	Okay.
Father:	Right, yeah.

[pause]

tone

Now you'll hear Part Four again.

[The recording is repeated.]

[pause]

That is the end of Part Four.
There'll now be a pause of five minutes for you to copy your answers onto the separate answer sheet.
I'll remind you when there's one minute left, so that you're sure to finish in time.

[pause]

You have one more minute left.

[pause]

That's the end of the test. Please stop now. Your supervisor will now collect all the question papers and answer sheets.
Goodbye.

Book 2 Test 2 Key

Paper 1 Reading

Part 1
1 E   2 G   3 A   4 D   5 H   6 F   7 B

Part 2
8 B   9 C   10 A   11 C   12 C   13 D   14 B

Part 3
15 B   16 F   17 A   18 G   19 D   20 H
21 C

Part 4
22 D   23 E   24 C   25 B   26 A   27 C
28 A   29 F   30 B   31 E   32 A   33 B
34 D   35 A

Paper 3 Use of English

Award one mark for each correct answer, except in Part 3, where two marks are available, divided up as shown, for each answer.

Correct spelling is essential throughout. Ignore omission or abuse of capital letters. No half marks.

Part 1
1 C   2 B   3 D   4 A   5 B   6 D   7 C   8 A
9 D   10 D   11 B   12 C   13 B   14 D   15 A

Part 2
16 away   17 so   18 a   19 without   20 whole
21 everyone/everybody   22 what   23 if/when   24 something
25 in   26 for/to   27 up   28 which   29 how   30 to

Part 3
31 would/'d have difficulty (1) (in) finishing (1)
32 still lives in Spain(,) (1) does (1)
33 the meeting (1) without saying (1)
34 don't/wouldn't mind (1) lending (1)
35 is/'s rare for (1) Angus to (1)
36 my fault (1) we didn't/did not (1)
37 you have (1) (any) plans for (1)

38 doesn't take (1) after (1)
39 isn't/is not as/so (1) good as (1)
40 I hadn't/had not (1) given Dennis (1)

Part 4

41 through   42 ✓   43 it   44 rather   45 anything   46 own
47 ✓   48 at   49 ✓   50 so   51 how   52 is   53 because
54 up   55 me

Part 5

56 beings   57 selection   58 applicants   59 advice
60 unsuccessful   61 Similarly   62 inadequate   63 confidence
64 ability   65 honesty

Paper 4 Listening

Part 1

1 A   2 C   3 B   4 C   5 B   6 C   7 A   8 B

Part 2

9 careers   10 overseas/in other countries/abroad
11 visit companies (and)/businesses   12 (are) homeless
13 (student) common room   14 hot meals
15 (a) book exchange (throughout the college)
16 (a student) advice centre   17 accommodation   18 speakers

Part 3

19 E   20 B   21 D   22 A   23 F

Part 4

24 B   25 C   26 A   27 B   28 C   29 A   30 A

Transcript   *First Certificate Practice Test Two. Paper Four. Listening. Hello. I'm going to give you the instructions for this test. I'll introduce each part of the test and give you time to look at the questions. At the start of each piece, you'll hear this sound:*

tone

You'll hear each piece twice.
Remember, while you're listening, write your answers on the question paper. You'll have time at the end of the test to copy your answers onto the separate answer sheet.

The tape will now be stopped. Please ask any questions now, because you must not speak during the test.

[pause]

PART 1   *Now, open your question paper and look at Part One.*
You'll hear people talking in eight different situations. For questions 1 to 8,
choose the best answer, A, B or C.

Question 1   One
This woman is talking on the telephone. Who is she speaking to?
A   *her landlord*
B   *an architect*
C   *a builder*

[pause]

tone

Woman: I, um, I've looked up my copy of the thing I signed when I came here, and it's quite clear. I'm responsible for keeping things clean and so on, but it is up to you to see that it gets painted and things when necessary . . . No, it's not that. I'm not just asking because I want to change the colour scheme. The window frames will start to rot if you don't do it soon . . . Well, that's up to you, but I think you ought to have another look . . .

[pause]

tone

[The recording is repeated.]

[pause]

Question 2   Two
On holiday, you hear another tourist describing a journey. How did he feel?
A   *shocked*
B   *embarrassed*
C   *scared*

[pause]

tone

Man: Anyway, they said it was very pretty, and well worth it because of the view up there. So, off we went, up that little road you can see from behind the hotel. And it wasn't a particularly good road anyway, and then we started twisting and turning about – ooh – and we were looking down into people's gardens and it felt – well, I just felt like we were going to go straight across their roofs half the time. I suppose you could get used to it if you grew up here, but not me. And coming down was even worse.

[pause]

tone

[The recording is repeated.]

[pause]

Question 3   Three
You hear these people talking in a café. Why did the man change his
newspaper?
A the cost
B the opinions
C the quality of the writing

[pause]

tone

Woman:	That's not the paper you used to get, is it?
Man:	No.
Woman:	I wondered who they'd attract by price-cutting.
Man:	Ha ha. All ten pence of it. But I was getting tired of their attitude. It's very narrow.
Woman:	Oh. How?
Man:	Well, at least they look at more than one side of things in this, even if it isn't as well-written, on the whole.

[pause]

tone

[The recording is repeated.]

[pause]

Question 4   Four
This woman is phoning a friend about the date of a meeting. Why has she
called?
A to apologise for changing it
B to inform her about changing it
C to explain the reason for changing it

[pause]

tone

Woman: It's about having to change the date of the committee meeting. I know you weren't best pleased about it, but the thing is, we've checked round and it really is the only date everyone can make. So that's got to be it really. I thought if you knew why, perhaps you wouldn't mind so much.

[pause]

tone

[The recording is repeated.]

[pause]

Question 5   Five
You hear a girl talking about clothes. What is she describing?
A a coat
B a dress
C a trouser suit

[pause]

tone

Girl: It was really a classic. It was in, um, this really soft, fine material, you know what I mean? And this incredible dark blue. There's a little, thin belt and it goes in tight at the waist and then it falls in these really deep folds – almost to the ankles. And then at the top – ooh – it's sleeveless and very plain, cut quite loose, but really beautifully finished.

[pause]

tone

[The recording is repeated.]

[pause]

Question 6 *Six*
Listen to this film critic. What does he like least about the film?
A the characters
B the action scenes
C the main story

[pause]

tone

Critic: I enjoyed it actually. It's not trying to be too clever. It's a straightforward adventure film with a, well, to be honest, pretty dull story, but it's well-acted. There's some sharp talking which is actually quite funny, a quite original car chase and a touching little love story woven through it. A pleasant way to relax for an hour or two if you get the opportunity, but not one to make a special trip for.

[pause]

tone

[The recording is repeated.]

[pause]

Question 7 *Seven*
You hear these people talking while queuing in a shop. What does the woman complain about?
A the payment system
B the service
C the quality of the goods

[pause]

tone

Man: It's nearly ten minutes.
Woman: Oh, but it's much better than it was.
Man: Honestly, I thought things would have improved more than this. I mean there's not much of a range, is there?

Woman:	What gets me, is why you still have to wait in line to choose things and then you have to wait in line again to pay. But you know, the people are much more relaxed and they try to help if they can.
Man:	Mm.

[pause]

tone

[The recording is repeated.]

[pause]

Question 8   *Eight*
You hear these people talking about a book. Who is the book about?
A a poet
B a songwriter
C a journalist

[pause]

tone

Male teenager:	. . . but it doesn't really tell you what he was trying to say.
Female teenager:	Yes, it does. It's got all those letters and stuff. You can see that's where the ideas for the words came from.
Male:	Yeah, okay. But what about the tunes? He practically doesn't mention them.
Female:	And that piece in the paper said they're the most original part of his work.
Male:	I don't know. I suppose the writer didn't know so he just left out talking about them.

[pause]

tone

[The recording is repeated.]

[pause]

That's the end of Part One.
Now turn to Part Two.

PART 2   *You will hear two students who want to be chosen as student representative in their college. For questions 9 to 18, complete the notes. You will need to write a word or a short phrase.*
You now have forty-five seconds in which to look at Part Two.

[pause]

tone

Linda:	Right, well, my name's Linda Goodyear and I'd like briefly to tell you why I think you should choose me as your rep. Um, these are the things I would try to do something about, try to improve, or, I mean, do.
	So, er, I think we all know, the careers advice service needs, er, a bit of improvement. So I'd work to improve that. Especially, we need more practical advice

about getting work experience, not in this country I mean, overseas. And another thing I think we should press for, is to have close links with businesses and companies where we can actually go on visits. I think we should try to get around, I mean not even just locally, but all over the Midlands, so we actually see a greater variety of ways of doing things rather than just hearing about them.

Then, um, the next thing I think is important is something I'm quite, er, involved with, myself. That's voluntary work with the homeless. I'd like to get more people here in the college involved, either directly, or I hope, with raising money.

And, er, last of all, er, I'd like to push the college authorities really hard for some new furniture for the student common room.

Thank you very much. Please vote for me.

Darren:	Hi, everybody. Uh, I expect you may know, my name's Darren Whiting. Um, I'd really like to be your student rep this year, and well, here's what I'd try and do for you, for us. Um, first, I'd take on the canteen and try to stop them putting up the price of hot meals, as they've said they will.

Then, the next thing is, um, well, I'd like to organise a book exchange throughout the whole college, um, like already exists, um, in the maths department, to save money on expensive textbooks that we all have to have, but don't need for the whole course. Another thing we badly need in this college is a student advice centre. We need a place run by students for students, where people can drop in and get advice about any sort of problems, academic or welfare or whatever.

We also need to take on the college authorities on the subject of accommodation for students who need it. I mean, the situation at the moment is crazy, with no proper system for deciding who gets accommodation, or why. I want to change that. And lastly, I want to get in more speakers, from all political backgrounds, and er, from industry and so on, to help get people more aware of, you know, what's going on in the world today. Because we'll all be out there soon, like it or not.

Please vote for me. Thanks for listening.

[pause]

tone

Now you'll hear Part Two again.

[The recording is repeated.]

[pause]

That's the end of Part Two.
Now turn to Part Three.

PART 3   *You will hear five people talking about sport.*
For questions 19 to 23, choose from the list A to F what they say. Use the letters only once. There is one extra letter which you do not need to use. You now have thirty seconds in which to look at Part Three.

[pause]

tone

Man:	As you can imagine, this job involves spending most of my time alone, sitting at the word processor. So, I try and get up to the tennis club once or twice a week. I just want

to move about a bit, make sure my legs and arms are still working. Doesn't really matter who I play with, most people are about the same standard. I really feel the difference if I miss a week though.

[pause]

Man: I don't really claim to be much of an expert. But at the end of the working week, I watch a good match on the box, or even go along to the local ground sometimes, and it just helps you forget all the stresses and strains, takes you out of yourself, you know what I mean?

[pause]

Woman: I don't think it was actually part of my original job description as such. When I started, someone said could I coach the under elevens sometimes, and I said yes, and somehow I've just gone on doing it, taking them to their matches and stuff. It's quite a pleasant change really, keeps me on the go, you know, once or twice a week.

[pause]

Boy: I, er my family moved here quite recently and, er, I didn't really bother much with sport before, but, um, I thought perhaps if I went along to this sports centre, you know, I could get to know a few different people from just the ones I see at school. Well, I quite enjoy it really, and I'm beginning to have a bit of a social life there as well, and I feel fitter too, which is an added bonus.

[pause]

Girl: It's a real laugh. We usually go every Saturday, and we wait outside and try to get a discount if we can. And we sometimes go round afterwards and try and get autographs. Well, that depends who's been playing of course. We all get worked up and have a good shout and get sore throats. It wouldn't be any good on your own, would it?

[pause]

tone

Now you'll hear Part Three again.

[The recording is repeated.]

[pause]

That's the end of Part Three.
Now turn to Part Four.

PART 4 *You will hear a local radio report about places to eat. For questions 24 to 30 choose the best answer A, B or C.*
You will have one minute in which to look at Part Four.

[pause]

tone

Presenter: And now that review of, er, local restaurants and suchlike where you might like to take the family over the bank holiday period. Caroline Chandler has been out and about sampling the goodies.

Caroline:	Yes, I'm going to be dieting for weeks!
Presenter:	So what have you found for us?
Caroline:	Well, I've been to all sorts of places, so I hope there'll be something of interest for everyone. Starting at the bargain end, I went to Ali's sandwiches in Long Road. Ali does a great trade at lunchtimes, normally he's got office workers queuing out of the front door. He says he'll be open over the holiday weekend, and he's offering take-away picnic packs as well. You need to phone in your order for these the previous day, then you can collect first thing in the morning if you're having a day out. The number's double seven, double five, three two.
Presenter:	And I'll be giving that phone number again at the end of the programme. So who's next, Caroline?
Caroline:	Okay. Well, next I tried Chick'n'things, on the Market Square. This was down on my list as a fast food shop, and I must admit I thought it might be cheap and greasy. But at least, I thought, this'll be a good place for a quick something hot to eat on the way home from the cinema. What I found was, it's not particularly cheap, but the food's really quite tasty, so it's not in fact bad value. The main thing you have to remember though, is it's not actually all that fast, because they cook each order separately, so you have to hang about a bit . . .
Presenter:	Right. So, what about if I want to sit down and eat?
Caroline:	Well, I decided to go through a day, trying to find a different place for each meal!
Presenter:	So, where did you have breakfast?
Caroline:	Well, I'd always heard that the best breakfasts are the ones they give those long distance lorry drivers at transport cafés. So, I got up at six o'clock and drove out to Pat's Café on the bypass just north of town. I got a very friendly welcome and a free mug of tea, and then had the biggest meal I've ever eaten. It was brilliant!
Presenter:	Well done!
Caroline:	The only thing was, I had to postpone the rest of my research till the next day because I simply hadn't got room for any more.
Presenter:	I guess that's one of the dangers of being a food journalist.
Caroline:	I guess it is. Anyway, the next day I decided to start cautiously. I went for morning coffee to the Old Mill in Riverside Park. I have to say it wasn't the best I've ever had. It was instant, okay, well, that's a matter of opinion, but still. Anyway it was very pleasant sitting looking at the river, and I thought, I'd better have something to eat, just a light cake, you know. Again, I'm afraid it was just very sweet and artificial-tasting. I suppose they don't have to try so hard because people go to the park anyway, but I think it's a real pity.
Presenter:	I know what you mean. Specially as it's so popular with tourists. It gives them just the wrong impression, doesn't it?
Caroline:	Yes, anyway, after that I wanted something a bit healthier, and luckily I was heading for the Food Box. Do you know it?
Presenter:	It's on the corner of Orchard Street, isn't it? I must admit I thought the food might be a bit dull, all salads and vegetarian pies, and I'd feel about twenty years older than all the other customers.
Caroline:	Well, I think you're missing a treat. They've got a great range of stuff. Okay, no meat, but really you won't miss it, there are so many tasty hot and cold dishes. And people of all ages go there. I have to admit I'm a regular, so I know what I'm talking about.
Presenter:	Okay, perhaps I'll try it next time I'm passing, you never know. And so where did you have dinner?

Caroline:	Ah, well, for dinner I went to the new Italian restaurant on Castle Street, the Four Seasons.
Presenter:	And?
Caroline:	It was brilliant! We were a bit late, because we were ages trying to find somewhere to leave the car –
Presenter:	Yes, I know, I've had the same trouble in that part of town.
Caroline:	But they didn't mind a bit, nothing was too much trouble, and the food – I could talk about nothing else the whole of the next day. Yummy!
Presenter:	Well, Caroline, we're coming up to news time so I'll have to say thank you, and quickly give the number for Ali's picnic packs as I promised . . .

[pause]

tone

Now you'll hear Part Four again.

[The recording is repeated.]

[pause]

That is the end of Part Four.

There'll now be a pause of five minutes for you to copy your answers onto the separate answer sheet. I'll remind you when there's one minute left, so that you're sure to finish in time.

[pause]

You have one more minute left.

[pause]

That's the end of the test. Please stop now. Your supervisor will now collect all the question papers and answer sheets.
Goodbye.

Book 2 Test 3 Key

Paper 1 Reading

Part 1
1 C   2 E   3 G   4 B   5 A   6 D

Part 2
7 C   8 A   9 B   10 D   11 C   12 D   13 A   14 B

Part 3
15 F   16 D   17 A   18 G   19 E   20 C

Part 4
21 B   22 E   23 A   24 G   25 E   26 and 27 D/F
28 A   29 D   30 C   31 A   32 B   33 and 34 D/E
35 G
(Where there are two possible answers, these are interchangeable.)

Paper 3 Use of English

Award one mark for each correct answer, except in Part 3, where two marks are available, divided up as shown, for each answer.
    Correct spelling is essential throughout. Ignore omission or abuse of capital letters. No half marks.

Part 1
1 B   2 C   3 D   4 D   5 C   6 B   7 A   8 C   9 B
10 B   11 C   12 A   13 C   14 A   15 B

Part 2
16 as/when   17 at/to/toward(s)   18 in   19 one
20 nothing/little   21 as   22 has   23 well   24 on   25 ago
26 up   27 no   28 were/was   29 make/form   30 every

Part 3
31 don't feel like (1) spending (1)
32 best match (1) I have/'ve (ever) (1)
33 look up (1) to (1)
34 there was (1) anything she wanted (1)
35 in case Sally (1) doesn't/does not (1)
36 we had (1) remembered to take (1)
37 there was nothing OR nothing was (1) wrong (1)

38 in spite of (1) the/a change (1)
39 'd/had (1) better think (1)
40 time Jackie (1) went swimming (1)

Part 4

41 the   **42** if   **43** so   **44** ✓   **45** it   **46** through
47 was   **48** in   **49** ✓   **50** for   **51** ✓   **52** being   **53** has
54 ever   **55** ✓

Part 5

56 development   **57** activities   **58** frequently   **59** behaviour
60 encourage   **61** imagination   **62** unexpected   **63** explanation
64 relating/related   **65** knowledge

Paper 4 Listening

Part 1

1 A   **2** B   **3** B   **4** C   **5** A   **6** C   **7** A   **8** A

Part 2

9 Studio Design Centre   **10** (his) mother's family   **11** engines
12 liners/ships   **13** physics   **14** post office (queue)   **15** clay
16 temperatures   **17** (wall and floor) tiles   **18** outdoors

Part 3

19 D   **20** E   **21** C   **22** F   **23** B

Part 4

24 Y   **25** N   **26** Y   **27** N   **28** Y   **29** Y   **30** N

Transcript   *First Certificate Practice Test Three. Paper Four. Listening. Hello. I'm going to give you the instructions for this test. I'll introduce each part of the test and give you time to look at the questions. At the start of each piece, you'll hear this sound:*

tone

You'll hear each piece twice.
Remember, while you're listening, write your answers on the question paper. You'll have time at the end of the test to copy your answers onto the separate answer sheet.
The tape will now be stopped. Please ask any questions now, because you must not speak during the test.

[pause]

PART 1   *Now open your question paper and look at Part One.*
You'll hear people talking in eight different situations. For questions 1 to 8,
choose the best answer, A, B or C.

Question 1   One
Listen to these colleagues talking. Why is the man going to Amsterdam?
A *on a business trip*
B *for a short holiday*
C *to study art*

[pause]

tone

Woman: Amsterdam, huh? Some people have all the luck. I've always wanted to do the museums there.

Man: Yeah, but you've got to remember I'm supposed to produce a guidebook at the end of it. My timetable won't let me enjoy the paintings – I'll be too busy checking which bus route they're on, and studying the price of souvenirs.

[pause]

tone

[The recording is repeated.]

[pause]

Question 2   Two
You're in a shop when you hear one of the assistants talking. What is he trying to do?
A *persuade someone*
B *explain something*
C *correct a wrong idea*

[pause]

tone

Shop assistant: Now, if I could just show you – a lot of people find it confusing. You see, these are what we call showerproof. They're what most people want. They'll keep out most of the wet, but they are what we call fashion garments, so – but nice, aren't they? But we do also have actual waterproofs too. But, um, they are more expensive. Well, if they're famous labels, anyway. So it depends really on how often you might get caught in a real rain storm, if you see what I mean?

[pause]

tone

[The recording is repeated.]

[pause]

Question 3   *Three*
You hear this reporter on the radio. Who is she going to meet?
A *a fisherman*
B *a scientist*
C *a farmer*

[pause]

tone

Reporter: Well, in recent years we've heard a lot about the damage to rivers and their fish stocks caused by pollution from agriculture. We've also been told that new laws have more or less put a stop to this kind of damage. Well, local fishermen say the farming community is ignoring them. So, I've asked pollution expert Dan Knox to meet me here on the river bank to carry out tests to see whether we can support the claims of either farmers or fishermen.

[pause]

tone

[The recording is repeated.]

[pause]

Question 4   *Four*
Listen to this teacher talking to a student. What is he giving?
A *some advice*
B *an opinion*
C *some information*

[pause]

tone

Teacher: Now, I'm no great expert on exactly what's around nowadays –
Student: Oh.
Teacher: But I do know that there's an enormous variety. There are full-time schools, and ones that only operate in the summer. There are intensive courses and others which are just a holiday with a few lessons thrown in.
Student: I see.
Teacher: There is a file of leaflets in the library.
Student: Oh, is there? I will look at them. Eh, thank you.
Teacher: You're welcome.

[pause]

Question 5   *Five*
You hear this critic talking about an exhibition. What is its subject?
A *life in a city*
B *the work of an architect*
C *rich and poor countries*

[pause]

tone

Critic: . . . and what I find most interesting, about what Pamela Eston has done, is to link together such a variety of images of the city, from, um, different stages, as it were, in its development. So that you get a feeling, um, of what living there's been like over the past five decades, and how that experience has changed. You know, she's got architect's plans and sketches from the fifties, alongside photos of present day homeless people, sheltering in the doorways of those same buildings.

[pause]

tone

[The recording is repeated.]

[pause]

Question 6 *Six*
You are listening to the news on the radio. Why was Brian Bolter on trial?
A for illegal gambling
B for accepting bribes
C for bribing players

[pause]

tone

Newsreader: . . . And news just in. Brian Bolter, the football manager accused of making illegal payments to players in order to fix the results of matches on which he had placed bets has been cleared of all charges. We're going straight over now to our correspondent outside the courtroom.

[pause]

tone

[The recording is repeated.]

[pause]

Question 7 *Seven*
You are on a bus when you hear this passenger get on. What does the driver offer to do?
A tell her when the bus reaches her stop
B point out the library
C stop outside the library

[pause]

tone

Passenger: Allard Road, please.
Driver: Which end?
Passenger: Um, I don't know. I want to go to the library.

Driver:	That's the top you want then. Fifty p . . . Ta. The stop's just up the hill from it. I'll let you know which one.
Passenger:	Oh, thank you.

[pause]

tone

[The recording is repeated.]

[pause]

Question 8   *Eight*
Listen to this boy talking about the town he lives in. What does he feel about it?
A He likes it.
B It's boring.
C It's old-fashioned.

[pause]

tone

Teenager:	Yeah, I don't think my Dad and Mum like it here any more. When I was little, it was just a sleepy old market town. We all liked it then. But now there's, um, a lot of commercial development, specially electronics and such, so it's changed a lot. They don't feel at home here like they did. But me, I've changed too. I've just about got a job lined up for when I leave school. I do think my parents would like to move really, but they know what I'd feel about that, so they'll probably stay – until I leave school, anyway.

[pause]

tone

[The recording is repeated.]

[pause]

That's the end of Part One.
Now turn to Part Two.

PART 2   *You will hear a radio journalist interviewing Frank Irvine, a successful potter. For questions 9 to 18, complete the notes. You will need to write a word or a short phrase.*
You now have forty-five seconds in which to look at Part Two.

[pause]

tone

Journalist:	Now, I'm with Frank Irvine whose current exhibition here at the Studio Design Centre in North London is attracting quite a bit of attention. And about time too, I should think. Um, Frank, I hope you won't mind my saying, but you're not all that young to be having a first major show in London?
Frank:	No, it's quite true. I was born in 1948, after all.

Journalist:	In Glasgow, was that?
Frank:	Actually no. My father was Austrian and I was born there.
Journalist:	Really?
Frank:	But my father died while I was still a baby and my mother, who was a Scot, returned with me to be near her own family.
Journalist:	Ah. And when did you start getting interested in making pots?
Frank:	Well, as a child I was into engines in a big way. Anything noisy and smelly, my mother would say. And out of that I developed an ambition to work in the shipyards.
Journalist:	Oh, did you?
Frank:	I wanted to be solving design problems with some of those great liners they used to build. A bit late in the day perhaps. I even started a degree in physics, um, at Edinburgh. But I think by the time I was about twenty I was already aware that there might be something else I wanted to do. I didn't know what, that's all.
Journalist:	So, what did you do?
Frank:	Well, I started travelling. Er, initially, to find out more about my father's background, and then I went to the Middle East and on to India. Where I met my wife, Carole.
Journalist:	And her father, I believe?
Frank:	Yes. We were all waiting in the post office in um, Bombay, actually, and we just struck up a conversation. And soon after that we came back to England and I was visiting them quite a lot and seeing her father working –
Journalist:	He being the potter Arthur Saunders –
Frank:	Right. Sorry. And eventually I plucked up courage to ask if I could have a go. And well, once I'd started, of course, I couldn't stop. I soon got very interested in experimenting with different kinds of clay.
Journalist:	From all over the world.
Frank:	Yes, that's right. And then I started playing around with patterns and colours and using very, very high temperatures to produce some pretty unique effects.
Journalist:	And this was quite some time ago?
Frank:	Oh, I've been playing about with this since the 1970s. I started with quite small bowls, you know, small domestic objects, then I wanted to try making designs on a larger scale, but still something that might find its way into a home, rather than a museum, so I tried wall tiles. You know, the sort of thing you can stick up in the kitchen or bathroom. Then I got onto the idea of them being used outdoors, like on patios and so on, so they got bigger and bigger. And other people like them too.
Journalist:	They certainly do. And I can see why.

[pause]

tone

Now you'll hear Part Two again.

[The recording is repeated.]

[pause]

That's the end of Part Two.
Now turn to Part Three.

PART 3   *You will hear five people being interviewed about how they spend their free time.*
For questions 19 to 23, choose from the list of activities A to F. Use the letters only once. There is one extra letter which you do not need to use. You now have thirty seconds in which to look at Part Three.

[pause]

tone

Interviewer: And in your free time?
Woman: When I have any! Well, I suppose it'll be better after I take the exam. But, well, I try to go to a club where there is a quite big pool I can use –
Interviewer: Uh-huh.
Woman: – and, eh, I try to do perhaps fifty lengths twice a week, I think it's one of the best ways –
Interviewer: Sure.
Woman: But that's all, at the moment, really.

[pause]

Interviewer: And how do you relax?
Man: I like to drive up into the hills with a sketch-book in my pocket.
Interviewer: Yeah?
Man: I like the idea of walking, but I soon get bored, or tired, so –
Interviewer: Yes.
Man: – I soon find a sheltered corner with a nice view and try to get it on paper.

[pause]

Interviewer: So what do you do?
Boy: I belong to this Youth Club, see?
Interviewer: Yeah?
Boy: And we put plays on and, you know, things –
Interviewer: You take part in them?
Boy: Well, just little parts so far. But we might do, like, a rock musical next year and I'm after something, the main bad guy, in that. You don't have to do any singing in it, luckily. It'd be really good.

[pause]

Interviewer: And how do you relax?
Woman: When I can –
Interviewer: Of course.
Woman: – now I don't have to regard feeding people as a duty –
Interviewer: Not day in, day out.
Woman: Right. I love to have a few friends round at the weekend, then spend lots of time dreaming up a menu, try out new dishes, see what they think. It's a nice change.

[pause]

Interviewer: And what's your ideal way to spend free time?
Man: Uh, I get out a pair of good old boots I had since college, and uh, just head on out into the country.

Interviewer:	Yeah?
Man:	I like to spend a while wandering around.
Interviewer:	Alone?
Man:	Yeah. But I like to take a break and talk to the locals sometimes. It's the only way to meet genuine country people, get out there and find them. And I get some good exercise, clear my head.

[pause]

tone

Now you'll hear Part Three again.

[The recording is repeated.]

[pause]

That's the end of Part Three.
Now turn to Part Four.

PART 4 *You will hear part of a radio documentary about running a small business. For questions 24 to 30, decide whether the idea was stated or not and mark Y for Yes, or N for No.*
You now have forty-five seconds in which to look at Part Four.

[pause]

tone

Presenter:	Lastly today on *Talking Shop* we're looking into getting started. You'd like to be your own boss? Well, you certainly need to look before you leap. John Apsley is the manager of a high street bank in the north of England.
John:	There are quite a lot of people who just aren't suited to running their own business. I get a lot of people come to me wanting a start-up loan. They haven't got a clue. They haven't studied their market. They haven't got a business plan. It's not enough if their friends like their home-made cakes, or their computer game or whatever. I tell them to go away and do their homework. It sounds hard, but I'm doing them a good turn. If they're any good, they'll be back. If not, well, we're both better off.
Presenter:	So what do you do? Sally has a T-shirt shop in Wilton.
Sally:	I went to see my Dad's accountant. She was a big help, didn't, like, just make me feel stupid, like he does sometimes. And she told me how to set things out, like a business plan, you know, to impress the bank manager. And he was, I think. Dad says he can be really fierce, but he was very helpful to me and I got lots of advice and a loan.
Presenter:	Otherwise . . . ? Megan Bracewell.
Megan:	It took me years to realise I wasn't really earning a living, because my paperwork was such a mess. You know, I was just bashing on, turning out the goods, and I'd never done any real costing. I didn't know how. Then I got this enormous tax bill. It nearly finished us off completely, about three years ago. Anyway, we just about managed to pay it, but it gave us such a fright, we had a big shake up and I think we've survived. But only just!
Presenter:	And if you do have problems? John Apsley again.
John:	Another thing is they don't get in touch before there's a crisis. They just sit there, watching it develop, and then come rushing round when, likely as not, there's nothing

more to be done. Then of course it's the bank's fault. But we can't help if the guy's not keeping us properly up to date, can we?

Presenter: As Colin Sharpe discovered.

Colin: I had this big export order. I phoned the bank, and I said, look, I've got this big order. It's the biggest I've ever had. I need to buy in a lot more raw materials, quickly like. Can I have some more credit? And they said, er, er, look at the file, basically no, you're extended as far as you can. It's too much of a risk. Course what I didn't tell them was who this customer was. Didn't occur to me that that might make a difference, did it? Then I just happened to see the assistant manager that evening, I was having a bit of a moan at him, and he says, who did you say? Course we'll be able to help you – just in time – ridiculous!

Presenter: Of course it helps to have a good relationship with the bank. But what else really matters? When you're working from dawn to dusk just to get the product out to the customers, it's difficult to find the time to attend to the other little details – John Apsley.

John: My clients in the computer world may not thank me for saying this, but you don't need all kinds of fancy systems to run a small business. What you need is to follow a simple routine and keep records. I'd rather see a single notebook and a shoe box full of receipts which are used every day than some expensive accounting software that nobody's had time to keep up to date.

Presenter: Well, that's telling you, as they say. Next week, we'll be looking at the subject of employment . . .

[pause]

tone

Now you'll hear Part Four again.

[The recording is repeated.]

[pause]

That is the end of Part Four.

There'll now be a pause of five minutes for you to copy your answers onto the separate answer sheet.
I'll remind you when there's one minute left, so that you're sure to finish in time.

[pause]

You have one more minute left.

[pause]

That's the end of the test. Please stop now. Your supervisor will now collect all the question papers and answer sheets.
Goodbye.

Book 2 Test 4 Key

Paper 1 Reading

Part 1
1 C   2 E   3 A   4 H   5 G   6 B   7 D

Part 2
8 B   9 D   10 B   11 D   12 C   13 A   14 A

Part 3
15 C   16 H   17 A   18 D   19 G   20 E   21 B

Part 4
22 B   23 G   24 D   25 G   26 F   27 A   28 D
29 C   30 A   31 G   32 E   33 G   34 D   35 B

Paper 3 Use of English

Award one mark for each correct answer, except in Part 3, where two marks are available, divided up as shown, for each answer.

    Correct spelling is essential throughout. Ignore omission or abuse of capital letters. No half marks.

Part 1
1 D   2 B   3 A   4 C   5 A   6 A   7 D   8 B   9 A
10 C   11 B   12 B   13 D   14 C   15 A

Part 2
16 side   17 may/might/could/would   18 As   19 known
20 the/his/this   21 made   22 if   23 of   24 its   25 there
26 brought   27 where   28 who/that   29 Until/Till/Before
30 to/onto/into

Part 3
31 said a/one word (1) to me (1) OR told me (1) a single)/one word (1)
32 didn't appear (1) to be (1)
33 had to (1) turn it down (1)
34 advised Carl (1) not to trust (1)
35 have no/haven't any idea (1) why (1)
36 the cheapest desk (1) you have (1)
37 was being (1) examined by (1)
38 make him (1) wash (1)

39 miss getting/receiving (1) letters (1); [miss hearing = 1 mark]
40 is expected (1) to accept (1)

Part 4

41 ✓   **42** past   **43** at   **44** those   **45** up   **46** must
47 just   **48** ✓   **49** same   **50** they   **51** ✓   **52** an
53 own   **54** very   **55** from

Part 5

56 decision   **57** professional   **58** photography   **59** reasonably
60 allowance   **61** agency   **62** useful   **63** sales   **64** original
65 publisher('s)

Paper 4 Listening

Part 1

1 A   **2** B   **3** C   **4** B   **5** A   **6** C   **7** C   **8** A

Part 2

9 (a) couple (of)/two/2   **10** bee-keeping   **11** (the) harbour
12 transport   **13** iron   **14** photographs   **15** soft play area
16 adventure playground   **17** science   **18** Fire and Flames

Part 3

19 F   **20** B   **21** C   **22** A   **23** D

Part 4

24 F   **25** T   **26** T   **27** F   **28** T   **29** F   **30** T

Transcript   *First Certificate Practice Test Four. Paper Four. Listening. Hello. I'm going to give you the instructions for this test. I'll introduce each part of the test and give you time to look at the questions. At the start of each piece, you'll hear this sound:*

tone

You'll hear each piece twice.
Remember, while you're listening, write your answers on the question paper. You'll have time at the end of the test to copy your answers onto the separate answer sheet.
The tape will now be stopped. Please ask any questions now, because you must not speak during the test.

[pause]

Now open your question paper and look at Part One.

PART 1 *You'll hear people talking in eight different situations. For questions 1 to 8, choose the best answer, A, B or C.*

Question 1 *One*
You hear this man talking on the radio about a politician. When did he get to know her?
A at school
B at university
C in his first job

[pause]

tone

Man: When I was at university, um, I'd hear of her from her cousins and things. She was, oh, travelling round the world at that time – making a name for herself already. She sounded very grand and successful to me. Yup, I found it hard to connect such a person with the girl – I used to help her with her homework, you know. Huh. And then she invited me to join the team she was putting together for her first election. I was very excited that she even remembered me. But I don't see so much of her now.

[pause]

tone

[The recording is repeated.]

[pause]

Question 2 *Two*
You're in a restaurant when you overhear this conversation. What is wrong with the food?
A It's stale.
B It's overcooked.
C It's the wrong order.

[pause]

tone

Mother: I'm afraid I must ask you to change my daughter's meal.
Waitress: Madam?
Mother: She can't eat this pizza. It's absolutely rock hard. It must've been sitting at the back of the oven all day.
Waitress: I'm very sorry. I can't think how it can have happened. I'll get another straight away.
Mother: Thank you so much.

[pause]

tone

[The recording is repeated.]

[pause]

Question 3   Three
You hear the weather forecast on the radio. How long will the bad weather
last?
A until midday tomorrow
B until tomorrow evening
C until the day after tomorrow

[pause]

tone

Weatherman: And, oh dear, here is a warning of severe weather conditions affecting the whole
country. Starting tonight, violent storms will reach all northerly regions by the end of
tomorrow morning and elsewhere in the country by the end of the day. They will
continue for a further twenty-four hours at least, with high winds and very heavy rain.
Storm damage is likely in hilly areas and drivers of high-sided vehicles should avoid
exposed roads and bridges. So do take care, won't you?

[pause]

tone

[The recording is repeated.]

[pause]

Question 4   Four
You are in a bank when you hear this conversation. What does the woman
want to do?
A borrow some money
B take out some of her money
C transfer her money to a new account

[pause]

tone

Customer: Um, it's about my savings account . . .
Cashier: Yes?
Customer: What I was wondering is whether there's any reason why I can't withdraw some money
from it before the end of the year. I mean, I know you're advised . . .
Cashier: Well, you'd lose interest of course, and you have to give a week's notice, but as long as
there's a minimum of hundred pounds left in, it's no problem.
Customer: Oh, right, well in that case, can I give notice now for two hundred pounds?

[pause]

tone

[The recording is repeated.]

[pause]

Question 5   *Five*
Listen to this man describing a concert. What did he like about it?
A *the first part*
B *the songs*
C *the instrumental section*

[pause]

tone

Man: Oh, it was dreadful. You know, they had this group in the middle, doing these songs from the sixties. They were rubbish then, even. I don't know why they brought them back. And all the rest was just really poor quality sort of jazz stuff, no singing, no atmosphere. They'd started with a couple of classic tunes from the thirties, and I'd thought oh, this is quite promising, someone's thought out the programme here, but they hadn't. It just got worse and worse.

[pause]

tone

[The recording is repeated.]

[pause]

Question 6   *Six*
Listen to these language teachers. What may cause a problem for students, according to the woman?
A *violence*
B *prejudice*
C *loneliness*

[pause]

tone

Teacher 1:   But what better way to learn a language?
Teacher 2:   I know, but people's feelings can be important, too.
Teacher 1:   What? Racist attitudes? That's not really likely, is it?
Teacher 2:   You misunderstand me. I meant, er, they'll be a long way from home, often alone – they may find it pretty tough . . .
Teacher 1:   Well, any big city can be dangerous if you're not sensible but . . .
Teacher 2:   No, just emotionally, that's all I'm saying.

[pause]

tone

[The recording is repeated.]

[pause]

Question 7   *Seven*
Some friends are talking about a film. What does the boy emphasise about the director?
A She's Indian.
B She's a woman.
C She's young.

[pause]

tone

Girl: I thought it was a bit obvious. You know, coming to terms with a different way of life, Indian communities and stuff, I mean I know there aren't so many women doing that kind of thing . . .

Boy: No, I know what you mean, but what's interesting is, I mean, you know she's not just a woman, she's not much older than us. Did you know that?

Girl: Really? Wow, imagine me going to India and saying 'I want to make a film' – just like that!

[pause]

tone

[The recording is repeated.]

[pause]

Question 8   *Eight*
You hear this woman talking about a colleague on the phone. What has he done?
A passed his driving test
B bought a car
C started driving lessons

[pause]

tone

Woman: Yes . . . apparently, he'd failed several times . . . stopped talking about it, mm . . . seemed a bit mean . . . so last time he just put his hand in his pocket and 'happened' to find the car keys in it, know what I mean? . . . Yeah, passed last week, apparently . . . it was rather sweet, I thought . . . and his wife'll be relieved . . . no, she used to have to keep giving him lifts . . .

[pause]

tone

[The recording is repeated.]

[pause]

That's the end of Part One.
Now turn to Part Two.

PART 2 *You will hear a radio feature about the city of Bristol. For questions 9 to 18, complete the notes. You will need to write a word or a short phrase. You now have forty-five seconds in which to look at Part Two.*

[pause]

tone

Teresa: Hello again. This is Teresa Shaw with *Where Next?*, our weekly travel and leisure spot. This week I've been looking at the attractions of Bristol, in the west of England. This ancient seaport has a lot to recommend it.

First of all, I'd like to tell you about Ashton Court. Now this is a lovely old house set in 350 hectares of parkland only a couple of miles from the city centre. All sorts of events go on there, or you can just relax in the grounds. There's a Visitor Centre where you can learn about the history of the house and park, and if you like honey, you'll enjoy the exhibition about bee-keeping over the last one hundred years.

For a different kind of history, you can make your way to the Maritime Museum and the Industrial Museum, both in the harbour area of Bristol. The latter houses, among other things, a special collection of all sorts of means of transport, from horse-drawn carriages to a helicopter. And just along the road is the S.S. Great Britain, the revolutionary ocean-going iron ship built in Bristol in 1843. This is a unique opportunity to find out about life at sea a hundred and fifty years ago. Definitely not to be missed.

But if all that sounds a bit mechanical for your tastes, there's always the zoo. As well as many fascinating animals, the zoo offers a variety of special events from bird flying displays to treasure hunts to an exhibition by some of the world's top wildlife photographers. You can phone for a special events brochure from March onwards. For young children, there is a special soft play area, and for slightly older ones with extra energy to burn off, there's an adventure playground. There are plenty of places to picnic or you can eat at the Pelican Restaurant. Wheelchair users are made welcome too, I'm happy to say. And remember, by supporting the zoo, you're also supporting its vital conservation work.

Lastly, still with the theme of education made enjoyable, there's the Exploratory. This is the place for a really different day out. It's full of exhibits which offer the chance for hands-on experience of the world of science. Each exhibit is a simple experiment which you carry out for yourself. Learn about how sound works, how we see colours, play with electricity – safely, of course – and masses of other scientific topics. There are also special live shows and workshops, such as *Bubble Magic* and *Fire and Flames*. There's also a shop full of amazing books and toys. It's easy to reach . . .

[pause]

tone

Now you'll hear Part Two again.

[The recording is repeated.]

[pause]

That's the end of Part Two.
Now turn to Part Three.

PART 3 *You will hear five people talking about feelings they have experienced. For questions 19 to 23, choose from the list of feelings A to F. Use the letters only once. There is one extra letter which you do not need to use. You now have thirty seconds in which to look at Part Three.*

[pause]

tone

Man: Anyway, I jumped off the train and I was going as fast as I could along the platform, 'cause I had this interview and I thought I was going to miss the bus into town, you know. This old guy was getting out of the next carriage and I half bumped into him, and he said, 'Watch where you're going, young fellow' and I just shouted 'Oh push off' and ran on. And then I got to the interview, and there he was, behind the desk. God, it was awful. I just wanted the earth to open up and swallow me.

[pause]

Woman: We hadn't actually invited him, but we didn't mind too much at first. At first he was quite good, helping and things, but that soon wore off. And then he never seemed to have any money on him when we went out anywhere. And it's not as if he's short, he's got a good job. Then I found out he'd been making phone calls all round the world. I tell you, he's a complete waste of space. He won't get through our door again.

[pause]

Man: I was living in the States for a while, looking after this friend's house while he was away on a business trip. One night as I was just drifting off to sleep the doorbell went. I looked out of the window, couldn't see anyone, decided I'd dreamt it. Just getting back into bed when it rang again. Still no sign of anyone. It took ages to get off again and then it woke me again. By then I was in such a state I couldn't sleep at all. Just sat there with the light on all night. I never did find out what had caused it.

[pause]

Woman: When we were little, we used to spend the summer holidays with some cousins in France. It was a lovely opportunity for us, although we didn't really appreciate it as much as we should have at the time. Anyway, I once broke some old vase that was quite valuable, and everyone blamed the dogs. No one ever even suggested it might have been me, but I felt dreadful all that summer. They all thought I was ill, but it was just a bad conscience.

[pause]

Man: Yeah, the course was good. Some of the teachers are, you know, quite well-known people. The only thing was – well, I know I knew the other students but, um, I haven't actually been away on my own anywhere for so long. I kept reminding myself it was a great chance, I mean, I was lucky to be there – but all the time there was this clock inside of me, you know, telling me how much longer before I could be on my way back.

[pause]

tone

Now you'll hear Part Three again.

[The recording is repeated.]

[pause]

That's the end of Part Three.
Now turn to Part Four.

PART 4   *You will hear part of a radio interview with Sharon Walker, a young woman who has recently changed her career. For questions 24 to 30, decide whether the statements are true or false and mark **T** for True, or **F** for False. You now have forty-five seconds in which to look at Part Four.*

[pause]

tone

Interviewer:	So, Sharon, the big question, why did you decide to give up tennis?
Sharon:	Well, it wasn't just something that happened overnight, of course. But three years ago, I'd been playing in a lot of big competitions, and I was very tired, I wanted to get away and have a good rest.
Interviewer:	This was after the French Open?
Sharon:	That's right. And I realised that actually I couldn't in fact do that because I was already fixed to play in various places all round the world for months ahead and I just had to go on.
Interviewer:	And you did. And went on winning, too.
Sharon:	Yes. It was actually a very good year for me professionally. But I became increasingly aware that I was playing because I had to. I mean, when I was younger, I just loved it. Not just playing, I mean, but everything, the competition, the travel . . .
Interviewer:	And you made a lot of money, too, didn't you?
Sharon:	I was a millionaire at eighteen. But don't misunderstand me. I'd play matches again tomorrow if that was all there was to it. Just walk out onto the court and start playing. I mean, I do still like to get a game in every day if I can. But I was worn out by all the other stuff. Um, I think when you're just a kid, at first it's funny when you go out to get a burger and next day it's all in the papers. But as you mature, well, as I did, you begin to need the space to develop, to find out about who you are, to explore relationships. And that's hard to do when there's always some journalist ready to tell everyone who you've been seeing and what you said and did, when you're still only nineteen. You lose the right to a private life. So, in the end, I thought, okay, maybe I've got another ten years at the top – if I'm lucky, then I'll still be wondering who I am and I'll have lost that ten years before I even begin to find out.
Interviewer:	So you got out?
Sharon:	Yeah.
Interviewer:	And you had to put up with some fairly unkind comments.
Sharon:	Uh-huh. There were some pretty mean things in the papers, and even some other players, I guess they thought I'd let them down in some way. After all, I was kind of admitting that tennis might not be the most important thing in the world, and that wasn't something that they were ready to accept, but I wasn't saying anything about what they were doing, I was only doing what seemed right for me.
Interviewer:	Do you have many regrets?
Sharon:	Well, it'd be less than the truth if I said none at all. Of course there are times when I

wonder if I made a big mistake. But I have a good marriage, a lovely daughter and a job which I enjoy, so they never last more than a few moments.

Interviewer: Ah, yes, your daughter –

Sharon: Maisie.

Interviewer: Do you hope Maisie will be a tennis star one day? Will you encourage her?

Sharon: Um, that's a tricky one. I wouldn't discourage her, if she had talent. But it's getting more and more difficult to keep a balance. The level of competition is so high, and it starts so early now, I think it's very difficult for kids to hold on to a normal life if they're in serious training. So – let's say, I won't break my heart if she never gets further than the local club.

Interviewer: Sharon, thank you for talking to us.

Sharon: My pleasure.

[pause]

tone

Now you'll hear Part Four again.

[The recording is repeated.]

[pause]

That is the end of Part Four.
There'll now be a pause of five minutes for you to copy your answers onto the separate answer sheet.
I'll remind you when there's one minute left, so that you're sure to finish in time.

[pause]

You have one more minute left.

[pause]

That's the end of the test. Please stop now. Your supervisor will now collect all the question papers and answer sheets.

Goodbye.